STUDENT BOOK COMBO

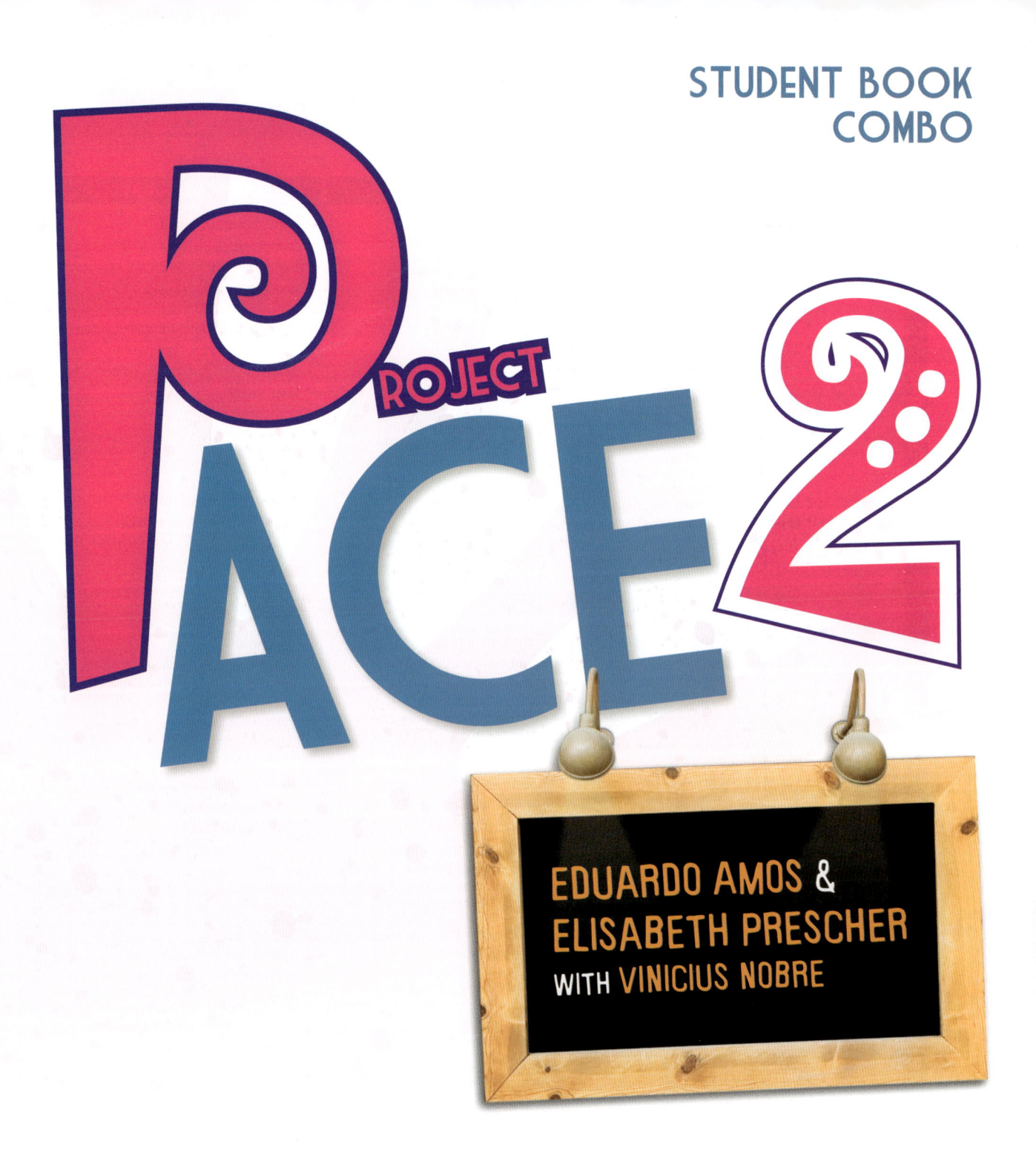

Project PACE 2

**EDUARDO AMOS &
ELISABETH PRESCHER**
WITH VINICIUS NOBRE

PEARSON
Longman

Scope & Sequence

	UNIT	LANGUAGE PATTERN	GRAMMAR	VOCABULARY
FIRST BIMESTER	**1** (pages 5–9)	• There is one apple. • There are five apples. • How many apples are there?	• There is / There are • How many • Plural of nouns ending in -s, -ss, -sh, -ch, -o, -x	• apple, banana, mango, orange, peach • bicycle, bus, car, dog, picnic table, tree, lake
	2 (pages 10–14)	• There is one girl in my class. • There are two girls in my class. • Is there a bank near here? Yes, there is. / No, there isn't. • Are there any banks near here? Yes, there are. / No there aren't.	• Is there?/Are there? • Prepositions: in, on, under	• calculator, CD, clock, computer, eraser • airport, aquarium, bank, casino, cathedral, garden, heliport, museum, palace • large, small,
		**Review Units 1–2** (pages 15–16)		
	3 (pages 17–22)	• How much is this sweater? / It is $9. • How much are these shoes? They are $20.50 • Can I help you?	• How much..? • Plural of nouns ending in -y • Plural review: word + -s, word + -es	• batteries, sunglasses, iPOd, watch, skateboard, motorbike • dollar, cent, change
		▶ **Pace Mix** (page 22)		
	4 (pages 23–27)	• She's the third person in line. • She's behind Bob.	• Prepositions of place: behind, between, in front of	• cute, person • ordinal numbers, cardinal numbers
		Review Units 3–4 (pages 28–29)		
		Project 1 (pages 30–31) **Tema Transversal: Work and Consumerism**		
SECOND BIMESTER	**5** (pages 32–37)	• Where's the post office? • Excuse me. • Thanks. / Thank you.	• Imperatives: go straight ahead turn right, turn left • Prepositions of place: next to, right across from, on, straight ahead, left	• school, post office, gas station, hotel, newsstand, drugstore, bookstore, block, lost
		▶ **Pace Mix** (page 37)		
	6 (pages 38–42)	• What can you do? I can dance. • Can you swim? Yes, I can. / No, I can't.	• Auxiliary verb: can • Connecting word: but	• play, speak, sing, dance, listen, run, swim • tennis, football, soccer, basketball. • piano, guitar, drums, violin • joke, volunteer
		Review Units 5–6 (pages 43–44)		
	7 (pages 45–50)	• Whose umbrella is this? It's Ana's. / It isn't Ana's. • Whose boots are these? They're Ana's.	• Question word: whose • Genitive (possessive)	• dress, pants, jacket, boots, tent, fish, back, • umbrella, keys, camera, tennis racket, • anything
		▶ **Pace Mix** (page 50)		
	8 (pages 51–55)	• What are you doing? I'm doing my homework.	• Present progressive	• talk, eat, draw, drink, read, look, help, listen, phone, write, run, look at, ask for, look like • neighborhood, gift, clothes • everything, everybody
		Review Units 7–8 (pages 56–57)		
		Project 2 (pages 58–59) **Tema Transversal: Health**		

UNIT	LANGUAGE PATTERN	GRAMMAR	VOCABULARY	
9 (pages 60–65)	• Do you like fish? Yes, I do. / No, I don't. • I like chicken. / I don't like fish. • I like him. / I don't like him.	• Simple present: like	• hamburger, taco, hot dog, fast food, sandwich, orange juice, milkshake, soda, coffee, milk, toast, cereal, French fries, soup, salad, beans, chicken, fish, eggs, rice	
➤ Pace Mix	(page 65)			
10 (pages 66–70)	• Open your mouth! • Don't open your mouth! • I like him. / I don't like him.	• Imperatives • Object pronouns: her, him	• body, head, neck, face, ear, mouth, shoulder, tongue, leg, nose, elbow, knee, foot, eye, arm, hand • touch, wake up, point, stretch, jump	THIRD BIMESTER
Review Units 9–10	(pages 71–72)			
11 (pages 73–78)	• Do they get up at 9:00? Yes, they do. / No, they don't. They get up at 7:00. / They don't get up at 6:00.	• Simple present: I, you, we	• get up, wash your face, brush your teeth, have breakfast/lunch/dinner, leave home, catch a bus, get to school, go to bed	
➤ Pace Mix	(page 78)			
12 (pages 79–83)	• He cooks. / He doesn't cook. • Does he / she cook…? Yes, he does. / No, he doesn't.	• Simple present: he/she • Spelling: third person singular	• read, do, cook, write, study, clean, run, wake up, build, watch, wash, go, love, begin, prepare	
Review Units 11–12	(pages 84–85)			
Project 3	(pages 86–87) **Tema Transversal: Multiculturalism**			
13 (pages 88–93)	• He has short arms and long legs. • Does it have a large beak? Yes, it does. / No, it doesn't.	• Simple present tense: have • Position of adjectives: size before color	• flamingo, beaver, turtle, antelope, crab, tiger, frog, snake, bald eagle, macaw, worm • wing, tail, pet, beak, horn, shell, teeth, fur, feather	
➤ Pace Mix	(page 93)			
14 (pages 94–98)	• Do you ever make your bed? Yes, I usually make my bed. No, I never do the dishes.	• Simple present contrasted with present progressive • Frequency adverbs: always, usually, ever, never	• set the table, make your bed, take out the garbage, do the dishes, take care of	FOURTH BIMESTER
Review Units 13–14	(pages 99–100)			
15 (pages 101–106)	• Where are you going? • How are you going? • When are you going?	• Review: question words	• train, plane, bus, car, boat • beach, mountains, movies, shopping mall • grandfather, grandmother, aunt, uncle, cousin	
➤ Pace Mix	(page 106)			
16 (pages 107–111)	• What are you doing? I'm looking for a present. • Where does he live? He lives in New York.	• Review: Present progressive • Review: Simple present	• tie, blouse, belt, post office, look for, teddy bear	
Review Units 15–16	(pages 112–113)			
Project 4	(pages 114–115) **Tema Transversal: Ethics**			

Workbook (pages 118–149) **Word List** (pages 150–154) **Grammar Reference** (pages 155–160)

©2009 by Pearson Education do Brasil

Todos os direitos reservados. Nenhuma parte desta publicação pode ser reproduzida ou retransmitida de qualquer modo ou por qualquer outro meio, eletrônico ou mecânico, incluindo fotocópia, gravação ou qualquer outro tipo de sistema de armazenamento e transmissão de informação, sem prévia autorização, por escrito, da Pearson Education do Brasil.

Autores: Eduardo Amos e Elisabeth Prescher com Vinícius Nobre
Gerente do Projeto: Albina Escobar
Gerente de Produção: Heber Lisboa
Editora: Kylie Mackin
Capa: Alexandre Mieda
Ilustrações: André Luiz de Souza Lima
Editoração Eletrônica: Figurativa Arte e Projeto editorial
Projeto Gráfico: Marcia Mauro
Impressão: São Paulo

Dados Internacionais de Catalogação na Publicação (CIP)
(Câmera Brasileira do Livro, SP, Brasil)

Amos, Eduardo
  Project Ace, 2 : student's book / Eduardo Amos, Elisabeth Prescher with Vinicius Nobre.
São Paulo : Pearson Education do Brasil, 2008.

  Inclui CD.
  ISBN 978-85-7659-231-0

  1. Inglês (Ensino fundamental) 2. Inglês (Ensino fundamental) – Problemas, exercícios etc.
  I. Prescher, Elisabeth. II. Nobre, Vinícius. III. Título.

08-04943   CDD-372.652

Índices para catálogo sistemático:

1. Inglês : Ensino fundamental   372.652

Agências fotográficas
p. 6 Maksymilian Skolik (1); Nanka (Kucherenko Olena) (2); g.lancia (3); angelo gilardelli (4); Dmitry Remesov (5); Kirsty Pargeter (6); **p.8** Berg Silva - Agência O Globo; **p.11** gibsons (1); Igor Smichkov (2); langdu (3); ayazad (4); © Helene Rogers / Alamy (5); PhotoCreate (6); AM-STUDIO (7); Marianne de Jong (8); Pavel Pustina (girl); Galina Barskaya (boy); **p.13** Vladimir Melnik; george green; **p.14** Douglas Freer; Lazar Mihai-Bogdan; **p.18** Kmitu; charles taylor; Dewayne Flowers; Germany Feng; SUE ASHE; artcalin; Lepro; aliciahh; Alexander Kalina; **p.19** Natalia Yakushkina; Clara Natoli; Marcus Miranda; skeletoriad; Tyler Olson; PhotoCreate; EHolmes; **p.20** Jozsef Szasz-Fabian (1); Bannykh Alexey Vladimirovich (2, 4, 6); Pakhnyushcha (3); R. MACKAY PHOTOGRAPHY (5); **p.21** Ximagination; Wolfgang Amri; Eleonora Kolomiyets; Mario Lopes; Ng Yin Jian; BelleMedia; **p.22** Poznyakov; Marc Dietrich; **p.28** Peter Guess (1); Iurii Konoval (2); Ljupco Smokovski (3); ArturKo (4); Eleonora Kolomiyets (5) © WoodyStock / Alamy (6) Cheryl Casey (7); Lepro (8); **p.30** Olexander Nerubayev; terekhov igor; Sarah Cates; Eleonora Kolomiyets; Dino O.; karen roach; Elnur; Shmeliova Natalia; Alexander Kalina; David Davis; Ronald Sumners; **p.31** Daniel Goodings; Radu Razvan; **p.33** © Joern Sackermann / Alamy (1); Sebastian Duda (2); Avesun (3); © RFR / Alamy (4); © Steve Skjold / Alamy (5); Pablo H Caridad (6); **p.36** titus manea; **p.37** Gabriela Trojanowska; Gregory James Van Raalte; **p.38** Yuri Arcurs; Rod Ferris; MaxFX; Gorilla; **p.39** (top) NeonLight (1); JoLin (2); Johann Helgason (3); Cristina CIOCHINA (4); (middle) Sergei Didyk (1); Lebedinski Vladislav (2); John Solie (3); Linux Patrol (4); (bottom) rj lerich (1); Tomasz Szymanski (2); Nick Stubbs (3); NIR KEIDAR (4); **p.41** Aleksandr Frolov (A); Teze (B); AYAKOVLEVdotCOM (C); Serghei Starus (D); **p.42** dr. Le Thanh Hung; **p.44** Galina Barskaya (1); PhotoCreate (2); Kruchankova Maya (3); PhotoCreate (4); kristian sekulic (5); Amy Myers (6); **p.45** keellia (1); Kalim (2); zimmytws (3); Morgan Lane Photography (4); Alexander Kalina (5); Eleonora Kolomiyets (6); Dino O. (7); Elnur (8); **p.46** (Kathy) Pchemyan Georgiy; Victoria Alexandrova; Eleonora Kolomiyets; Ivan Kruk; (David) Denis Pepin; Lezh; Pakhnyushcha; Blazej Maksym; (miriam) Dallas Events Inc; Eleonora Kolomiyets; Tatiana Popova; (Jaime) Wolfgang Amri; Feng Yu; Pablo Eder; **p.47** First Class Photos PTY LTD (1); terekhov igor (2); Marcelo Saavedra (3); pandapaw (4); Ingvald Kaldhussater (5); eszawa (6 e 7); STILLFX; (bottom) Alex Kosev; Tatiana Popova; BPlucinski; Tal Delbari; **p.48** Eleonora Kolomiyets (A e F); Olga Sweet (B); © Mode Images Limited / Alamy (C) PhotoCreate (D); Elisanth (E); **p.49** Tatiana Popova (1); PhotoCreate (2); Cheryl Kunde (3); Eleonora Kolomiyets (4); **p.50** Maxim Tupikov; **p.53** Sander Rom (1); MANDY GODBEHEAR (2); Diego Cervo (3); VR Photos (4); Ingrid Balabanova (5); Craig Foster (6); **p.54** Lisa F. Young (A); iofoto (B); Jose AS Reyes (C); © Mark Scheuern / Alamy (D); Jason Stitt (E); Hannamariah (F); **p.55** Losevsky Pavel; Natalia Bratslavsky; **p.56** Eleonora Kolomiyets; **p.59** MitarArt; **p.60** Jaren Jai Wicklund (left); Natalia Sannikova (middle); Junial Enterprises (right); **p.61** bouzou (1); Nassyrov Ruslan (2); Boris Ryaposov (3); Flashon Studio (4); Robert Milek (5); Lana Langlois (6); Lepas (7); Billy Gadbury (8); ukrphoto (9); Elke Dennis (10); artproem (11); Joao Virissimo (12); Maksymilian Skolik (13); Tamara Kulikova (14); **p.65** (top) Monkey Business Images; (bottom) MalibuBooks (1); elaine hudson (2); @erics (3); Orla (4); Graca Victoria (5); Gelpi (6); Stephen Strathdee (7) Ustyujanin (8); newphotoservice (9); Dmitriy Shironosov (10); **p.67** Melissa King; **p.68** Losevsky Pavel (1); kristian sekulic (2); Zoom Team (3); Kurhan (4); Denis and Yulia Pogostins (5); Andrejs Pidjass (6); **p.73** Khomulo Anna (1); Kuznetsov Alexey Andreevich (2); vahamrick (3); Tomasz Trojanowski (4); **p.75** Losevsky Pavel; **p.76** Lee Morris; **p.77** Dustin Mudry; **p.78** ArrowStudio, LLC; **p.80** Franziska Richter (1); rmj&lspn (2); Rudolf Polle (3); Peter Albrektsen (4); raluca teodorescu (5); Paul B. Moore (6); Lev Olkha (7); © Stefan Sollfors / Alamy (8); **p.82** Muriel Lasure; gingerlash; **p.84** Donald P Oehman; iofoto; Juriah Mosin; Adrian Britton; Paul B. Moore; Sasa Petkovic; Ronen; Perov Stanislav; Cynthia Farmer; **p.87** Entertainment Press; p.89 salamanderman; Mosista Pambudi; bpatt81; wong yu liang; Anke van Wyk; Timothey Kosachev; tororo reaction; Tony Campbell; Eric Isselée; Artem Illarionov; Alistair Michael Thomas; Sascha Burkard; Guryanov Oleg; Happy Alex; **p.90** serthorn (A); Olga Kushcheva (B); Reddogs (C); Sean Nel (D); Norman Bateman (E); Magdalena Bujak (F); **p.91** Marina Cano Trueba; Condor 36; beltsazar; Judy Worley; aliciahh; Stephen Meese; **p.93** Michael Pettigrew; **p.94** Christoph Weihs; Jaren Jai Wicklund; marilyn barbone; Photoroller; **p.95** Ulrike Hammerich; Geanina Bechea; fred goldstein; **p.97** Andrejs Pidjass; Hannamariah; Losevsky Pavel; iofoto; Andi Berger; **p.98** Philip Lange (1); Gabriel Moisa (2); Zsolt Nyulaszi (3); Simone van den Berg (4); **p.99** Bobby Deal / RealDealPhoto; **p.102** SexyGirls_Vehicles; erikdegraaf fotografie; L Kelly; julia-photo; Monkey Business Images; LEXX; Tomasz Trojanowski; **p.103** Petr Stalbovskiy; Christian Wheatley; Dmitriy Shironosov; **p.104** Audrey M Vasey; Morgan Lane Photography; **p.107** Wolfgang Amri; IgorXIII; Losevsky Pavel; Kalim; Kamil Fazrin Rauf; **p.108** James Steidl; Vasina Natalia; Norman Chan; Elnur; **p.109** Natalia Bratslavsky; **p.110** emin kuliyev; Sean Nel; **p.112** Thomas Barrat / egd (1); Andrey Parfyonov / Arvind Balaraman (2); Losevsky Pavel / Dino Ablakovic (3); Ricardo Manuel Silva de Sousa / magri (4); Melanie Lupoli / john330 (5); Dhoxax / Fesus Robert (6); **p.113** sabri deniz kizil (1 e 2); vnlit (3); Wolfgang Amri (4); Eleonora Kolomiyets (5); **p.114** GeoM; Glenda M. Powers (6); **p.119** Michael Kletnetsky; **p.133** Cristy (1); Indigo Fish (2); kristian sekulic (3); Andi Berger (4); max blain (5); Hallgerd (6); paulaphoto (7 e 8); **p.134** Maxim Bolotnikov (A); yuri4u80 (B); Randall Stevens (C); Stefan Glebowski (D); GeoM (E); iofoto (F, G); Cathleen Clapper (H); Kiselev Andrey Valerevich (I); Ramzi Hachicho (J); aida ricciardiello (K); Pinkcandy (L);

Agradecimentos
Agradecemos aos professores que participaram das pesquisas e/ou analisaram este material, em todo ou em parte, contribuindo para aprimorá-lo: Glenda Rabitsch, Fernanda Maciel Machado Horta, Cristiane Salles Tinoco, Vania Lopes, Wanice Gonzales Moreira, Glaucia Herandes Bezerra, Maria Cecilia Burgos Piotto, Janine de Melo Lima, Solange Gonçalves Diniz, Diana Augusta Costa Bacelar, Monica Claudia Alves Saraiva, Érika Koblitz Essinger, Josué Gomes, Elizabete Maria Simas de Sant'Anna, José Carlos da Silva, Alessandra Costa Fagundes, Janaína Rodrigues de Andrade, Juliana de Cássia Soares Diniz, Celeste Fernandes Belo, Adriana Dip Andreotii, Fernanda Junqueira Soares, Aryadne de França Carvalho, José Gomes de Oliveira Filho, Simone de Andrade Lima Santana, Miriam Andrade Ramos Bueno do Prado, Maria Cristina Antunes Braga, Gustavo Rodarte Boechat, Marlene Gomes de Aveliz, José Bernardo da Silva, Gisele Cristina Malhavaras, Mabel Cymbaluk, Velma R. Ross Gallone, Maria Regina Campos de Andrade, Alzira Maria Maluli Mendes, Gracielly Rodrigues, Maria Bethania Cavalcanti, Helena Camacho Pestana, Mariana Esteves, Renata Asano, Daniela Viveiros Fernandes.

Unit 1

There's a chocolate cake.

Listen and practice.
02

Mother: How many sandwiches are there?
Daughter: There are ... twelve ... No, there are fourteen.
Mother: How many sodas?
Daughter: Seven.
Mother: Is there enough food for everyone? How many kids are there?
Daughter: Well, there are seven kids.
Mother: Let me see ... fourteen sandwiches, seven sodas, apples ... . Oh, there's a chocolate cake, too. It's enough!
Daughter: Fine! All set for the picnic.

How many...?	→	Quantos / quantas...?
There is	→	Há
There are	→	Há

5

LESSON 1

SPEAKING

2 Listen and practice.

1.  apple — apples
2. orange — oranges
3. banana — bananas
4. peach — peaches
5. mango — mangoes
6. box — boxes

3 Read and practice.

Examples:

1. A: How many dogs are there?
   B: There's one dog.

2. A: How many cars are there?
   B: There are three cars.

Labels in picture: lake, bird, car, tree, bicycle, boy, dog, picnic table

4 Describe the picture in Exercise 3. Use *there is* and *there are*.

In the picture, there are _____

_____

_____

LESSON 2

5 **Look at the picture and practice the dialogs.**
Examples:
1. A: How many oranges are there?
   B: There are nine oranges.
2. A: How many birds are there?
   B: There's one bird.

LISTENING

6 **Look at the picture in Exercise 5. Listen and check True or False.**
03

	1	2	3	4	5	6	7	8	9	10
True										
False										

WRITING

7 **Look at the picture in Exercise 5 and write sentences.**
1. (peach) *There are three peaches.*
2. (box) _____
3. (mango) _____
4. (bird) _____
5. (apple) _____
6. (orange) _____

LESSON 2

READING

8 Read about Sítio Burle Marx, a special place in Rio de Janeiro.
04

SÍTIO BURLE MARX

Posted by Joey Rooth from Pittsburgh, PA on 08/29/2007

If you go to Rio, visit the charming *Sítio Burle Marx*.

Burle Marx was a famous Brazilian landscape designer. He was the first to use Brazilian flora in landscaping projects.

He lived on a *sítio* in Rio that is now a cultural center. On the *sítio*, there is an old farmhouse, a small colonial chapel, greenhouses and the Burle Marx studio. On the *sítio*, there are plants from all over the world — more than 3,500 species. There are also plants discovered by Burle Marx, and many plants that are on the endangered list.

Make a reservation: there are only 2 guided tours per day. Also, take a map.

I loved this place.

Address: Estrada Roberto Burle Marx 2019,
Rio de Janeiro, Brazil
Phone: 021/2410 – 1412

Open: Tues. – Sun.
Tours: 9:30 AM & 1:30 PM; by appointment only.

9 Check True or False.

	True	False
1. Burle Marx was not Brazilian.	___	___
2. There are greenhouses on the *sítio*.	___	___
3. There are plants from all over the world.	___	___
4. There are many chapels, too.	___	___
5. There is a new farmhouse.	___	___
6. Burle Marx is the name of a plant.	___	___

LESSON 3

10 **Answer the questions.**

1. Where is *sítio Burle Marx*? _____
2. What is the *sítio* now? _____
3. When is the *sítio* open? _____
4. How many guided tours are there per day? _____
5. How many species of plants are there? _____

WRITING

11 **Describe the picture.**

1. (apple) <u>There are two apples on the table.</u>
2. (book) _____
3. (pencil) _____
4. (mango) _____
5. (peach) _____

12 **Draw a place you like in your city and describe it.**

This is . . .

GRAMMAR

HOW MANY

Question
How many kids are there?

VERB
There to be (= haver)
There is one boy. (= Há)   **There are** two girls. (= Há)

PLURAL OF NOUNS
Nouns ending in **-s**, **-ss**, **-sh**, **-ch**, **-o**, **-x** : add **-es**
bus**es**   class**es**   brush**es**   peach**es**   potato**es**   box**es**

(See Grammar Reference, charts 1, 2, and 13, pages 155 and 160.)

VOCABULARY

bicycle	apple
bus	orange
car	banana
mango	lake
tree	peach
dog	picnic table
appointment	designer
endangered	farmhouse
chapel	greenhouse
guided tour	
enough	

Unit 2

There are twenty students.

1 Listen and practice.
05

Boy 1: How many students are there in your class this year?
Boy 2: There are thirty-four, I think.
Boy 1: Wow! It's pretty large. Mine's small. There are twenty students.
Boy 2: How many girls?
Boy 1: There's only one.
Boy 2: Are you serious?
Boy 1: I'm kidding. There are eleven girls.
Boy 2: Well, in my class there's only one boy. Me!
Boy 1: Are you serious?
Boy 2: Of course not! I'm kidding.

LESSON 1

SPEAKING

2 Listen and practice.

1. computer
2. calculator 
3. CD 
4. clock 
5. magazine 
6. eraser 
7. iPod 
8. stapler 

3 Look at the picture and practice.

Examples:

There is one computer on the desk.

There are three books under the chair.

LESSON 2

4 **Look at the picture and practice the dialogs.**

Examples:

1. A: Is there a book under the chair?
   B: Yes, there is. / No, there isn't.

2. A: Are there books on the desk?
   B: Yes, there are. / No, there aren't.

LISTENING

5 **Listen and number the pictures.**
06

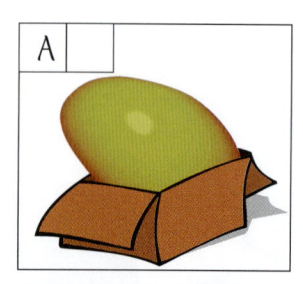

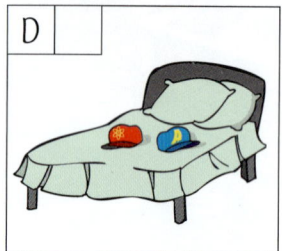

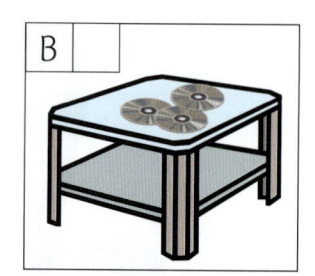

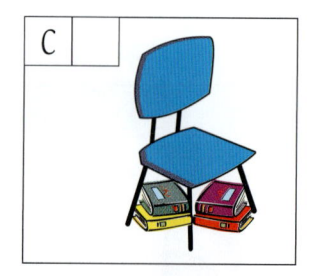

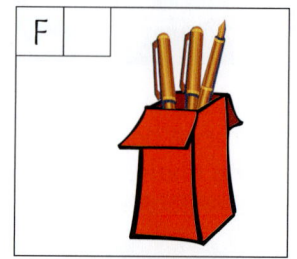

A B C
D E F

WRITING

6 **Describe the pictures in Exercise 5.**

Example:

There is one mango in the box.

LESSON 2

READING

7 Read about a very small country in Europe.
07

A SMALL COUNTRY

Principality of Monaco

Ruler: Prince Albert II (2005)

Area: 1.95 sq km

Location: on French Riviera on the Mediterranean

Capital: Monaco

Largest city: Monte Carlo

Currency: Euro

Languages: French (official), English, Italian, Monegasque or Monecan

Highways: 50 km

Airports: none

Heliports: 1

Not all the countries in the world are big. Some countries are smaller than Central Park in New York.

Monaco, officially Principality of Monaco, is the second smallest country on Earth and it is ruled by a prince. It is famous as a tourist and recreation center.

The main attractions are the Oceanographic Museum and the Aquarium, the Monaco Cathedral, the Prince's Palace, and some magnificent gardens.

The Principality is also popular for the famous Monte Carlo casino and for the Monaco Grand Prix.

LESSON 3

8 **Answer the questions.**

1. Are there highways in Monaco? _____
2. How many heliports are there in Monaco? _____
3. Where is Monaco? _____
4. What is the official language? _____
5. Is the cathedral in Monaco or in Monte Carlo? _____

9 **Underline and correct the mistakes.**

1. Monaco is ruled by a president. _____
2. There are five official languages in Monaco. _____
3. There is a famous palace in Monte Carlo. _____
4. Dollar is the currency. _____
5. There is an Oceanographic Palace in Monaco. _____
6. The Prince's palace is in Monte Carlo. _____

WRITING

10 **Describe your country. Use *there is* and *there are*.**

In Brazil, there are 26 states.

GRAMMAR

Question
Is there a bank near here? (Há um banco perto daqui?)

Are there any banks near here? (Há algum banco perto daqui?)

Answers
Yes, **there is**.
No, **there is not**.
          isn't.
Yes, **there are**.
No, **there are not**.
          aren't.

(See Grammar Reference, chart 1, page 155.)

VOCABULARY

eraser — calculator
CD — bank
magazine — computer
clock — small
large — airport
heliport — museum
aquarium — cathedral
palace — casino
garden — stapler

14

Review 1-2

1 Look at the picture and write questions for the answers. Use the words in the box.

1. _How many cars are there_ ? There is one.
2. _____ ? There are five.
3. _____ ? There are two.
4. _____ ? There is one.
5. _____ ? There are four.

car
dog
bicycle
bird
chair

2 Look at the picture again and describe it.

There is a swimming pool.

_____

_____

_____

3 Look at the picture and say where the objects are. Use *in*, *on*, or *under*.

1. (TV)   The TV is on the chair.
2. (books)   _____
3. (CD)   _____
4. (sweater) _____
5. (posters) _____
6. (sneakers) _____

4 Match the questions with the answers.

__c__ 1. Are the books on the floor?   a. Yes, it is.
_____ 2. Is the calculator on the desk?   b. There are three.
_____ 3. How many pens are there?   c. Yes, they are.
_____ 4. Where are the CDs?   d. They are under the chair.
_____ 5. Are the sneakers under the bed?   e. Yes, there is.
_____ 6. Is there a computer in your house?   f. No, they are not under the bed.

Unit 3

They're four dollars.

1 Listen and practice.
08

Salesperson: Hi! How can I help you?
Customer: How much is this CD, please?
Salesperson: It's twenty-two dollars fifty.
Customer: Hmm ... and how much are the AA batteries?
Salesperson: They're four dollars.
Customer: I want the CD and the batteries, please.
Salesperson: That's ... twenty-six dollars and fifty cents.
Customer: Here you are.
Salesperson: Here's your change, three dollars fifty.
Thank you. Have a nice day.

SPEAKING

2 Listen and practice.

one cent (penny)
five cents (nickel)
ten cents (dime)
twenty-five cents (quarter)
fifty cents (half-dollar)
twenty dollars
five dollars
one dollar
ten dollars

LESSON 1

3 Listen and practice.

1. 10¢
2. 35¢
3. 98¢
4. $1.50
5. $6
6. $7.99
7. $25.40
8. $36.75
9. $50.00
10. $84.25

4 Look at the picture and practice the dialogs.

| How much is...? | → | Quanto custa...? / Qual é o preço...? |
| How much are...? | → | Quanto custam...? / Qual é o preço...? |

Examples:

1. A: How much is this CD?
   B: It's ten dollars and fifty cents.

2. A: How much are these batteries?
   B: They're two dollars and seventy-five cents.

Summer Sale

- watch — $100.00
- CDs — $10.50
- batteries — $2.75
- calculator — $15
- skateboard — $21.00
- iPod — $90.90
- sunglasses — $25.90
- motorbike — $10,000

18

LESSON 2

5 **Look at the ad and practice the dialog.**

Example:

A: Can I help you?

B: How much is this pencil?

A: It's fifty cents.

B: OK. Two pencils, please.

A: That's one dollar altogether.

B: Here you are.

A: Thank you.

SPECIAL OFFERS!

$1.50
$1.35
$0.50
$2.50
$1.75
$20.00
$0.25

LESSON 2

LISTENING

6 Look at the items and price tags. Listen and check True or False.

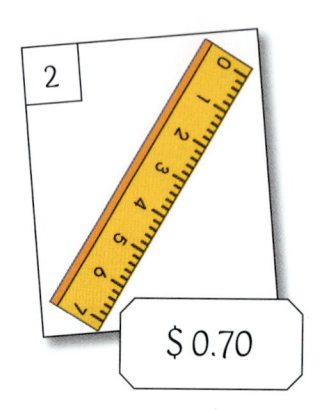

1. Batteries — $ 7.20
2. Ruler — $ 0.70
3. Notebook — $ 3.65
4. Pencil — $ 0.85
5. Eraser — $ 0.90
6. Pen — $ 2.80

	True	False
1.	✓	
2.		
3.		
4.		
5.		
6.		

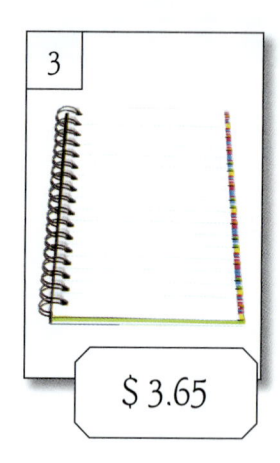

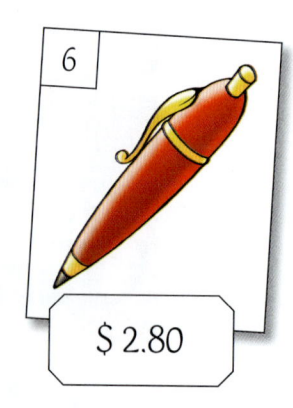

WRITING

7 Look at the items again and answer the questions.

1. How much is an eraser? _____
2. How much is a ruler? _____
3. How much is a pencil? _____
4. How much are the batteries? _____

8 Look at the items in Exercise 6 and write about the prices.

Example: Four batteries are $ 7.20.

1. two rulers
2. one notebook
3. four pencils
4. two erasers
5. three pens

LESSON 3

READING

9 **Read the ad and answer the questions.**

1. What day is the sale?
   Saturday.
2. How much are the flip-flops?
   _____
3. How much is the T-shirt?
   _____
4. What color are the shorts?
   _____
5. How much is the skirt?
   _____
6. How much is the bathing suit?
   _____
7. How much is the top?
   _____

SATURDAY SALE!!

$ 11.75
$ 6.95
$ 4.65
$ 10.35
$ 7.98
$ 5.85

10 **Write questions.**

1. _How much are the shorts?_ _____ They're $7.98.
2. _____ They're red.
3. _____ It's green.
4. _____ It's $6.95.
5. _____ They're blue.

WRITING

11 **Create an ad with five items. Ask questions to a friend.**

GRAMMAR

Questions		Answers
How much	is this sweater?	It is $ 9.
	are these shoes?	They are $ 20.50.

PLURAL OF NOUNS
Nouns ending in **–y**: change y to **ies**: baby – bab**ies**

PLURAL – REVIEW
words + -s: boy**s**, girl**s**, apple**s**, car**s**, etc.
words + -es: bus**es**, brush**es**, class**es**, church**es**, box**es**

VOCABULARY

glasses   battery
watch   money
skateboard   dollar (s)
iPod   cent (s)
change

Can I help you?
Have a nice day!

(See Grammar Reference, charts 2 and 13, pages 155 and 160.)

Pace Mix

NUMBER • 001 • APRIL

TONGUE TWISTER

How many cookies could a good cook cook if a good cook could cook cookies?

cookies: biscoitos
could: poderia
cook: cozinheiro/a
to cook: cozinhar

WORD SEARCH – find ten words

```
W N M U C H A M E H W D E Y
R W I C A L C U L A T O R I
A H U E R Q Y N A H Z L A E
D E L N G I S D A K I L S A
I R K T E P P E A C H A E S
O E V X N D S R N W O R R U
Y G B A T T E R Y H U P T E
```

EURO

The euro is the currency of 13 European Union countries: Belgium, Germany, Greece, Spain, France, Ireland, Italy, Luxembourg, the Netherlands, Austria, Portugal, Slovenia and Finland (since 1 January 2002).

As from 1 January 2008, the euro is also the currency of Cyprus and Malta.

currency: dinheiro
European Union: União Européia
since: desde

Unit 4

She's behind Bob.

1 Listen and practice. 🎧 10

Sally: See that girl over there?
Tim: Where?
Sally: Over there. The girl with long hair.
Tim: The one in front of Bob?
Sally: No, the one behind him.
She's between Bob and Jack.
She's the third in line.
Tim: Yeah, what about her?
Sally: She's Brazilian.
Tim: Really? She's cute. Is she your friend?
Sally: Yes. Come on! Let me introduce you.

SPEAKING

2 Listen and practice.

between   behind   in front of

3 Talk about your classmates. Use *behind*, *between* or *in front of*.
Example:
1. A: Is Marina behind Laura?
   B: No, she isn't. She's in front of Laura.

23

LESSON 1

4 **Listen and practice the ordinal numbers.**

1st: first	2nd: second	3rd: third	4th: fourth	5th: fifth
6th: sixth	7th: seventh	8th: eighth	9th: ninth	10th: tenth

5 **Look at the picture and practice the dialog.**

Example:
A: Who's the first person in line?
B: Linda is the first person in line.

Mike | Anna | Scott | Rebecca | Pat | Sam | Ron | Tony | Greg | Linda

WRITING

6 **Look at the picture in Exercise 5 and answer the questions.**

1. Is Tony the second person in line?   _No, he isn't. He's the third person in line._
2. Is Rebecca the fourth person in line? _____
3. Is Scott the eighth person in line? _____
4. Is Anna the ninth person in line? _____
5. Is Sam the tenth person in line? _____
6. Is Pat the fifth person in line? _____
7. Is Ron the third person in line? _____
8. Is Mike the sixth person in line? _____

LESSON 2

LISTENING

7 Listen and check the correct picture.
11

1. A  B  C
2. A  B  C
3. A  B  C
4. A  B  C
5. A  B  C
6. A B C

25

LESSON 2

READING

8 Read the text. Write the correct names in the boxes.

Lisa

Who Are They?

Nicole is behind Jeff. Her shorts are blue. She is the second in line.
He is the first in line. His pants and his shoes are brown. His name is Jeff.
She is behind Tony and in front of Matthew. Her hair is brown and her name is Lisa. Becky is between Nicole and Tony. Sylvia is the eighth in line. Greg is in front of Sylvia.

9 Answer the questions.

1. Who is the fourth person in line? _Tony is the fourth person in line._
2. Who is the sixth person in line? _____
3. Who is in front of Matthew? _____
4. Who is between Nicole and Tony? _____
5. He is between Matthew and Sylvia. What is his name? _____

10 Check True or False.

	T	F
1. Her shorts are blue. Her name is Nicole.	✓	___
2. There are eight people in line.	___	___
3. His pants are black. His name is Jeff.	___	___
4. Her dress is red. Her name is Becky.	___	___
5. Lisa is in front of Matthew and Greg.	___	___
6. His pants are green. His name is Greg.	___	___

LESSON 3

WRITING

11 Look at the picture. Write sentences to describe it.

1. (Andy / between) <u>Andy is between Telma and Yoshio.</u>
2. (Yoshio / in front of) _____
3. (Marina / behind) _____
4. (Telma / in front of) _____
5. (Wagner / behind) _____
6. (Marina / between) _____

12 Draw a map of the desks in your class and describe it.

Felipe is between Julia and Paulo.

GRAMMAR

PREPOSITIONS OF PLACE
between (= entre): I am **between** my brother and my sister.
behind (= atrás de): There is a cat **behind** the sofa.
in front of (= na frente de): The teacher is **in front of** Jack.

Cardinal numbers: 1 (one), 2 (two), 3 (three), etc.
Ordinal numbers: 1st (first), 2nd (second), 3rd (third), etc.

(See Grammar Reference, chart 3, page 155.)

VOCABULARY

person — sixth
first — seventh
second — eighth
third — ninth
fourth — tenth
fifth — in line
over there — cute
Let me introduce you.

Review 3-4

1 Look at the prices. Write the questions and the answers. Follow the example.

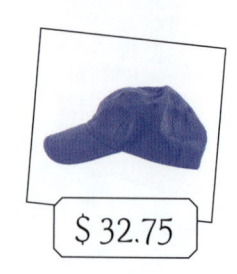

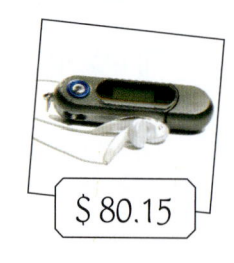

$ 78.25
$ 59.00
$ 6.50
$ 32.75
$ 120.00
$ 80.15
$ 34.90
$ 745.00

Example: (sunglasses)   How much are the sunglasses?
They are seventy-eight dollars and twenty-five cents.

1. (calculator) _____ ?
   _____ .

2. (cap) _____ ?
   _____ .

3. (jeans) _____ ?
   _____ .

4. (scooter) _____ ?
   _____ .

5. (watch) _____ ?
   _____ .

6. (Mp3 player) _____ ?
   _____ .

7. (batteries) _____ ?
   _____ .

2 Look at the music chart and write each singer's position. Use ordinal numbers.

MUSIC CHART
Top 10 - this month

#1 – Mariah Kerrin
#2 – Alicia Doors
#3 – Justin Timberriver
#4 – Chris Green
#5 – Britney Sports
#6 – Christina Matillera
#7 – Tijanna
#8 – Ni - Yu
...

1. Mariah Kerrin is the first singer on the chart.
2. _____
3. _____
4. _____
5. _____
6. _____
7. _____
8. _____

3 Look at the chart again. Write where each singer is on the chart. Use *between*, *in front of* or *behind*.

1. (Alicia Doors/between) Alicia Doors is between Mariah Kerrin and Justin Timberriver.
2. (Chris Green/in front of) _____.
3. (Tijanna/behind) _____.
4. (Britney Sports/between) _____.
5. (Ni-Yu/behind) _____.
6. (Christina Matillera/in front of) _____.
7. (Justin Timberriver/between) _____.
8. (Mariah Kerrin/in front of) _____.

4 Match the questions with the answers.

_____ 1. How many caps are there on the bed?
_____ 2. How much is this pen?
_____ 3. Is Joe behind Jenny?
_____ 4. How much are those shorts?
_____ 5. Are there any books under the chair?
_____ 6. Is Rosa in front of Liz?

a. Yes, she is.
b. No, he is in front of her.
c. Yes, there are.
d. There are three.
e. It's only fifty cents.
f. They're $34.

Project 1

WORK AND CONSUMERISM

Shopping on the Internet

1 Look at this web page and complete the sentences with the prices.

Shop online

- Electrical Goods
- Furniture
- Men
- Women
- Kids
- Sports
- Toys & Games
- Latest Offers

$ 34.90
$ 75.98
$ 87
$ 21.99
$ 14.90
$ 19.90
$ 15.99
$ 28.50
$ 42
$ 32
$ 43
$ 67
$ 15
$ 38.50

1. The sneakers are _____
2. The swimsuit is _____
3. The watch costs _____
4. The T-shirt costs _____
5. The shoes cost _____

Project

1. Go to the Internet and find two websites that sell clothes.
2. Make a list of ten items and their prices.
3. How can you pay?
4. What are the dangers of buying things on the Internet?

Shopping in stores

2 Make a list of the clothes you like.

_____   _____   _____
_____   _____   _____
_____   _____   _____

3 You are going shopping. Select five items to buy.

Project

1. With your list, go to a store in the neighborhood and ask for the prices.
2. How much do you need to buy these clothes?
3. Compare the prices with the ones on the website on page 30. Which prices are lower?

Unit 5

Go straight ahead.

1 Listen and practice. 🔊 13

Girl: Ned, we're lost. This is not Third Avenue.
Boy: Let me read this again.
Hmm ... go straight ahead for two blocks. Then, turn right on Third Avenue. The post office is next to the bank!
Girl: But look! There is no post office here!
Boy: You're right! Let's ask that police officer.
Girl: Excuse me, sir. Where's the post office?
Police Officer: Go ahead for one block. Turn left. The post office is across from the newsstand.
Girl: Thanks!
Police Officer: Have a nice day!

| next to | ➡ | ao lado de |
| across from | ➡ | em frente de (no outro lado da rua) |

SPEAKING

2 Listen and practice.

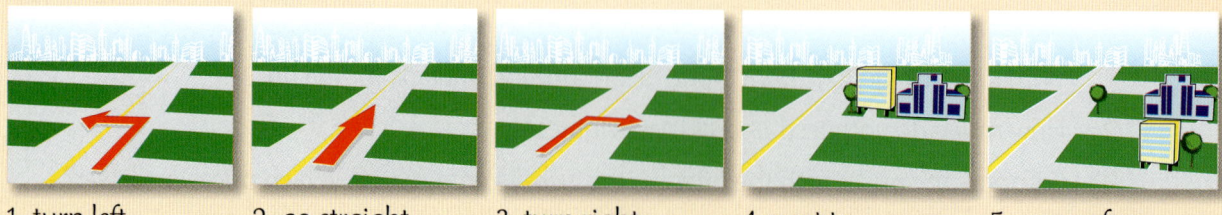

1. turn left
2. go straight ahead
3. turn right
4. next to
5. across from

LESSON 1

3 Listen and practice.

1. bookstore
2. drugstore 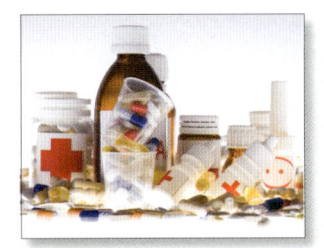
3. gas station 
4. school 
5. hotel 
6. post office 

4 Look at the map and practice the dialog.

Example:

A: Excuse me. Where's the hotel?
B: Go straight ahead for one block.
   Then turn left on Oak Street.
A: Turn left on Oak Street?
B: Yes. The hotel is across from the gas station.

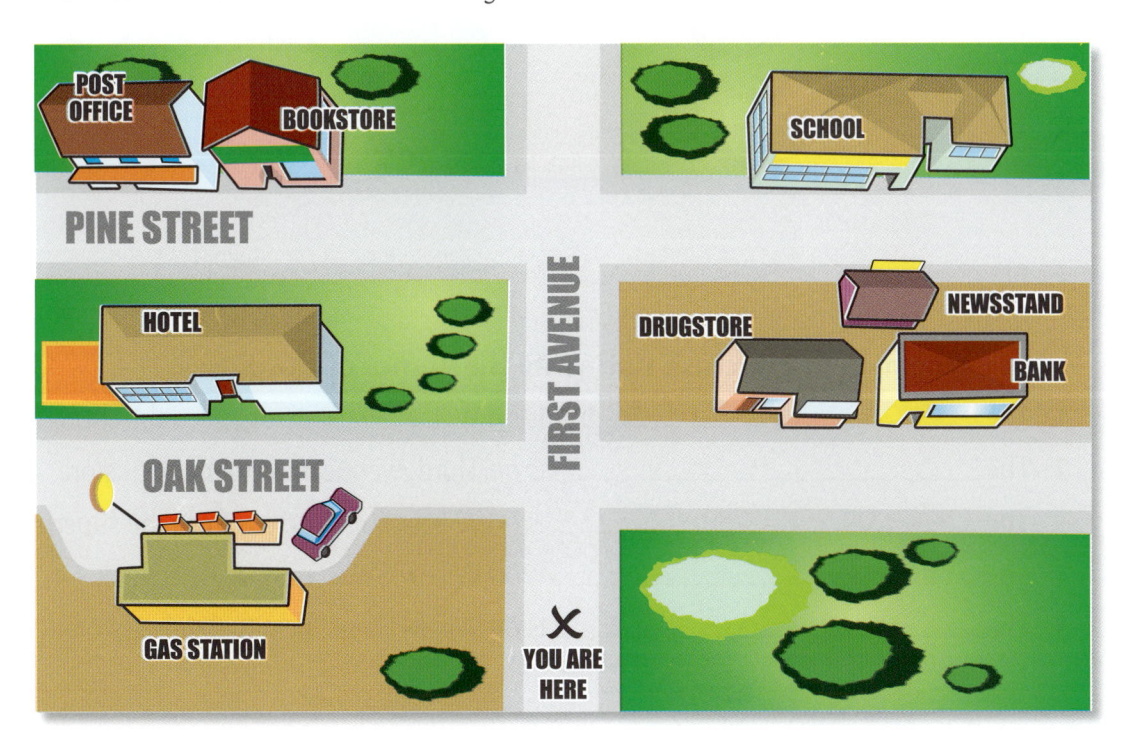

Lesson 2

5 Look at the map and practice the dialog.

Example:

A: Excuse me. Where's the church?

B: The church is on Willow Street, across from the bookstore.

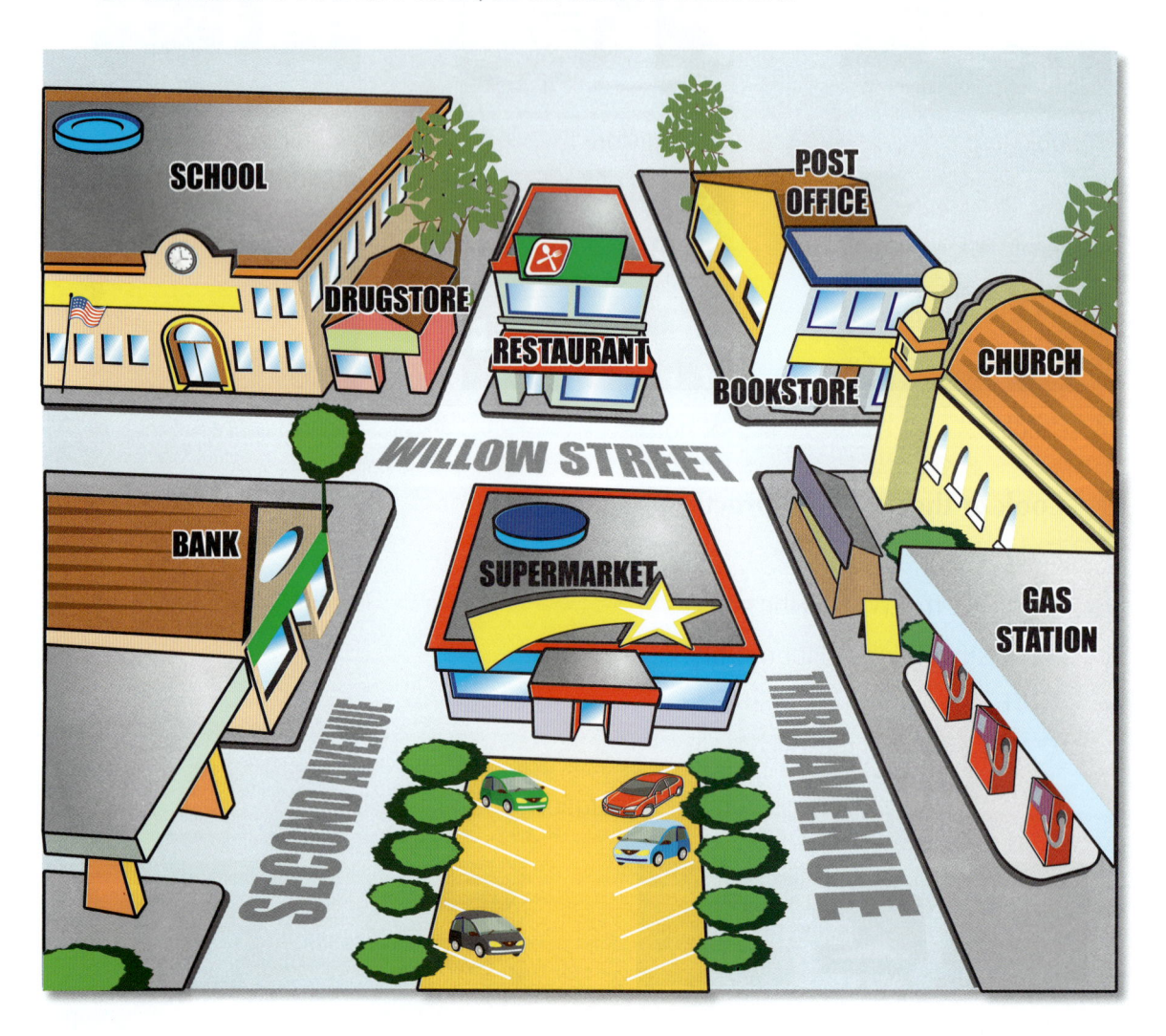

WRITING

6 Look at the map in Exercise 5 and write the names of the places.

1. The _____ is on Willow Street, across from the church.
2. The _____ is on Third Avenue, next to the bookstore.
3. The _____ is on Willow Street, across from the supermarket.
4. The _____ is on Willow Street, next to the school.
5. The _____ is on Willow Street, next to the drugstore.

LESSON 2

7 **Look at the map in Exercise 5. Write about these places.**

1. (school) _The school is next to the drugstore._
2. (bank) _____
3. (bookstore) _____
4. (post office) _____
5. (drugstore) _____
6. (church) _____
7. (gas station) _____
8. (supermarket) _____
9. (restaurant) _____

LISTENING

8 **Look at the map. Listen and check True or False.**

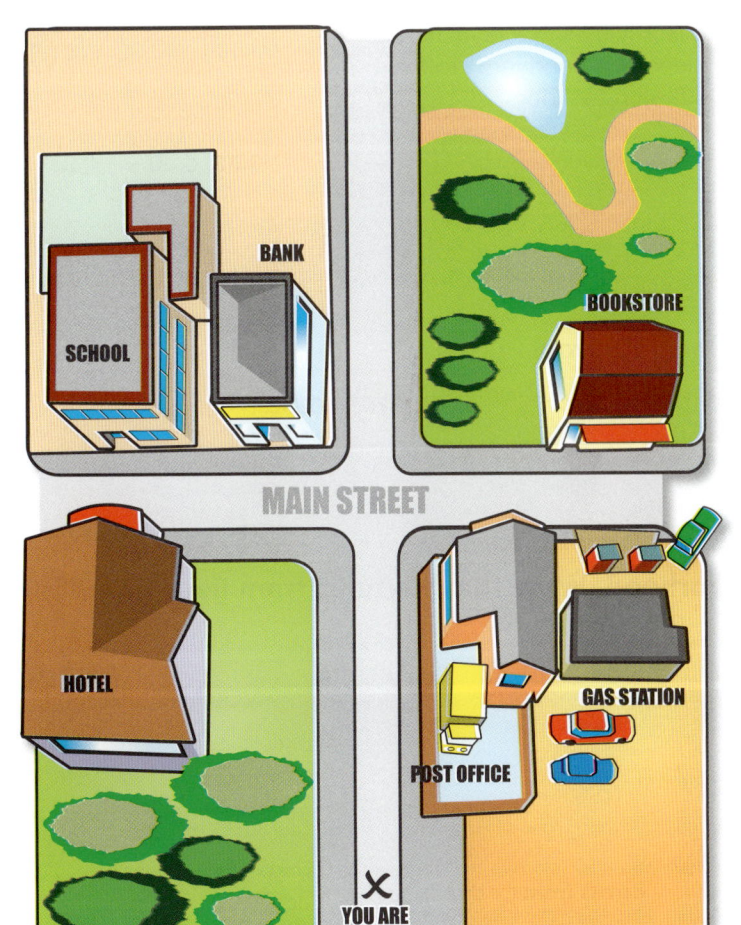

🎧 14

	True	False
1.		✓
2.		
3.		
4.		
5.		
6.		

35

LESSON 3

📑 READING

9 Read the information about famous places in Verona.
🎧 15

A few hours in Verona

We're going to spend a few hours in Verona. Any suggestions?
Mieko

- Visit Juliet's House on the right bank of the Adige River. Go to Piazza Erbe and then to Via Cappello. There is the House of Juliet with its famous balcony. In front of the house is a bronze statue of the girl. Continue along Via Leoni past Ponte Navi and the church of San Fermo Maggiore. Just a short walk away, next to an old convent, is the Tomb of Juliet.

Francesca

- Romeo's House is not far from Juliet's House. To go from one to the other, cross the Botanical Gardens. It is a typical medieval house with the construction arranged on three sides of a courtyard. To the left of the entrance, there is a stairway to the upper floors.

Toni

The famous balcony of Juliet

JULIET'S HOUSE

Via Cappello, 23

School groups: € 1,00

Entrance: € 4,00

Hours: 8:30 – 19:30

10 Read the texts again. Imagine and draw.

1. a map from the Adige river to the tomb.
2. Romeo's house.

✏️ WRITING

11 Draw a map of your neighborhood. Write the directions from your house to your school.

GRAMMAR

IMPERATIVES
Turn right.   Turn left.   Go straight ahead.

PREPOSITIONS OF PLACE
next to (= ao lado de): The hotel is **next to** the bank.
across from (= do outro lado da rua): The school is **across from** the church.
on (= na, em): Turn right **on** Pine Street.

(See Grammar Reference, charts 3 and 4, pages 155 and 156.)

VOCABULARY

school	drugstore
post office	bookstore
gas station	block
hotel	lost
newsstand	next to
left	right
across from	straight ahead

Pace Mix

NUMBER • 002 • MAY

How much is it?

code: 5 = e   6 = f   7 = g   8 = h   9 = i   20 = t   25 = y

It is 5 9 7 8 20
___ ___ ___ ___ ___ dollars

and 6 9 6 20 25
___ ___ ___ ___ ___ cents.

The Empire State Building

Address: 5th Avenue
City: New York City
State: New York
Country: U.S.A.

Height: 381 m (1,250 ft)
Floors: 102
Construction ended: 1931
Construction period: over 18 months.

Facts
The building incorporates 10 million bricks, 1,886 kilometres (1,172 miles) of elevator cables and 6,400 windows. There are 1,575 steps from the lobby to the 86th floor.

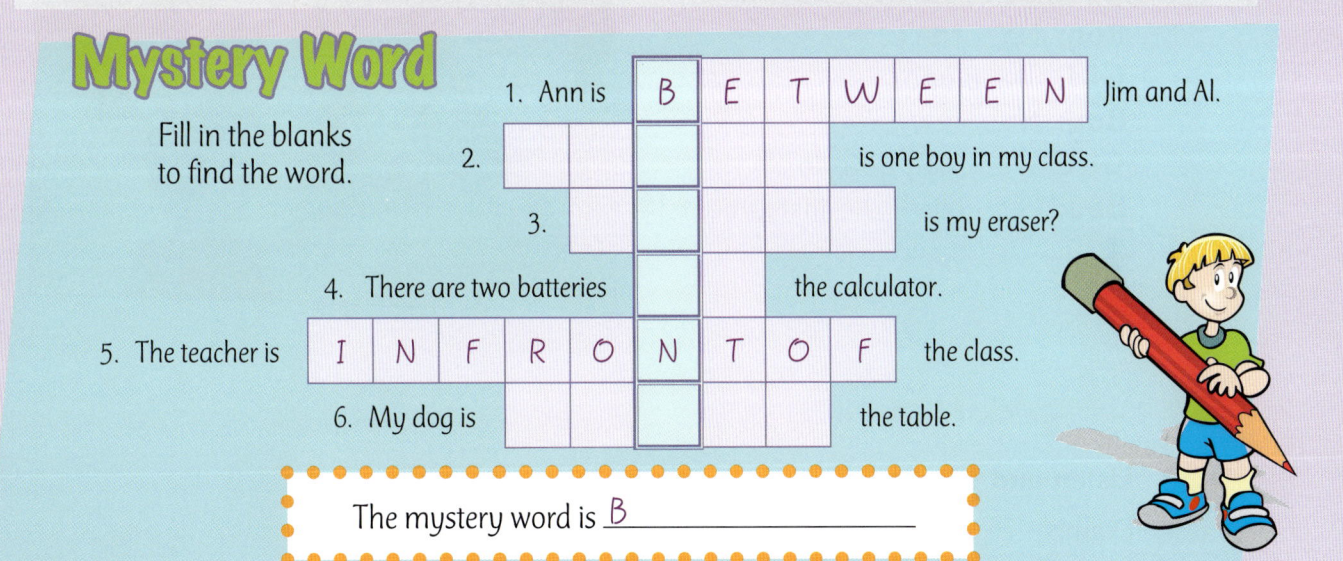

Mystery Word

Fill in the blanks to find the word.

1. Ann is B E T W E E N Jim and Al.
2. ___ is one boy in my class.
3. ___ is my eraser?
4. There are two batteries ___ the calculator.
5. The teacher is I N F R O N T O F the class.
6. My dog is ___ the table.

The mystery word is B_____

Washing Information - know the meaning of the symbols on your clothes!

- Cotton wash (wash at 60°)
- Wool wash (wash at 40°)
- Hand wash only
- Tumble dry 
- Do not tumble dry
- Dry flat
- Cool iron 
- Hot iron
- Do not iron

care: cuidado   cotton: algodão   wool: lã   iron: ferro   to wash: lavar   to tumble dry: centrifugar para secar   cool: frio   flat: estendido

For more information go to http://www.ariel.co.uk

Unit 6

I can play the guitar!

1 Listen and practice.
🎵 16

Girl: Can you sing, Joe?
Boy: No, I can't.
Girl: I can't, either, but I can play the guitar.
Boy: I can't.
Girl: Can you play the drums?
Boy: No, I can't...
Girl: The piano?
Boy: No...
Girl: What can you do?
Boy: I can carry the instruments!

SPEAKING

2 Listen and practice.

Example:
A: What can you do?
B: I can sing.

1. sing
2. swim 
3. dance 
4. run 

38

LESSON 1

3 **Look at the pictures and practice.**
Example:
A: Can you speak English?   B: Yes, I can.   C: No, I can't.

SPEAK ...

1.  English
2.  Spanish
3.  German
4.  Japanese

PLAY the...

1. piano
2. guitar 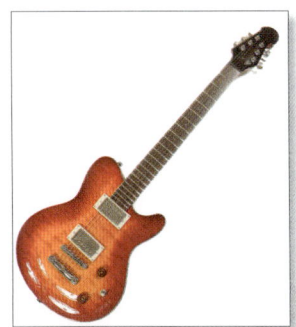
3. violin 
4. flute 

PLAY ...

1. soccer
2. football 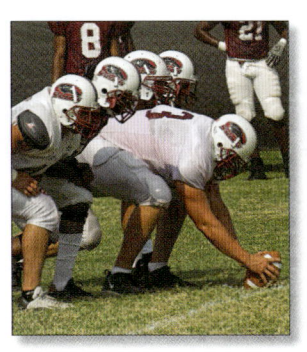
3. tennis 
4. basketball

LESSON 2

4 Look at the pictures and practice the dialogs.

Example:

A: Can they play football?
B: No, they can't.

A: Can she play basketball?
B: Yes, she can.

WRITING

5 Look at the pictures above. Write what the people *can* or *can't* do.

1. He can play basketball.
2. They can't play football.
3. _____
4. _____
5. _____
6. _____
7. _____
8. _____

6 Choose two friends. Write what they *can* and *can't* do.

Carla is my friend. She can ... She can't ...

LESSON 2

LISTENING

7 · 17 Listen and number the pictures.

A B C D

WRITING

8 Write about the people. Use *can*, *can't*, and *but*.

1. (he) He can run, but he can't sing.

2. (he) _____

3. (I) _____

4. (he) _____

5. (they) _____

41

LESSON 3

READING

9 Read the letter.

to Texas Children's Hospital

Dear Sirs,

My name is Alex Swanson. I am 13 and I am in the 7th grade. I know you need volunteers to help with the children in the hospital.
I can speak English and Spanish. I can play the guitar and the piano.
I can sing too, but not very well. I can play games and maybe, tell stories. You know, kids love stories! My favorite subject at school is math. But I am not bad at languages and reading. How can I help?
Yours,

Alex Swanson

10 Answer the questions.

1. How old is Alex? _He is thirteen_
2. What can he play? _____
3. Can he play games? _____
4. In your opinion, can he help? _____

11 Underline and correct the mistakes.

1. <u>There is a child</u> in the hospital.   _There are children in the hospital._
2. He can speak three languages.   _____
3. He cannot sing.   _____
4. He is bad at languages and reading.   _____

GRAMMAR
AUXILIARY VERB – can

Affirmative		Negative	
I		I	
You		You	
He / She / It	can	He / She / It	can't (cannot)
We		We	
They		They	

Questions	Answers
What **can** you do?	I **can** dance.
Can you swim?	Yes, I **can**. / No, I **can't**.

VOCABULARY

play	soccer
speak	basketball
sing	piano
dance	guitar
listen	violin
tennis	joke
football	drums
run	volunteer
help	swim
tell	

(See Grammar Reference, chart 5, page 156.)

Review 5-6

1 Look at the map and write T for true or F for false. If the sentence is false, correct the information.

1. The bank is next to the hospital. (F) _The supermarket is next to the hospital._
2. The church is across from the bookstore ( ) _____
3. The restaurant is across from the drugstore. ( ) _____
4. The supermarket is next to the school ( ) _____
5. The drugstore is on First Avenue. ( ) _____
6. The church is on Main Street. ( ) _____
7. The gas station is next to the restaurant. ( ) _____
8. The restaurant is on First Avenue. ( ) _____
9. The bank is next to the bookstore ( ) _____
10. The school is on Main Street. ( ) _____

2 Give directions from where you are to these places.

1. (school) _Go straight ahead for one block. Then turn right on Main Street._
2. (bookstore) _____
3. (hospital) _____
4. (gas station) _____
5. (bank) _____

43

3 Look at the pictures and cues. Write what people *can* and *can't* do.

1. play tennis

   She can't play tennis, but she can dance.

2. play baseball

   _____

3. swim

   _____

4. play soccer

   _____

5. play the guitar

   _____

6. dance

   _____

4 Underline the mistake and correct the sentence.

1. There is five apples on the table. There are five apples on the table.
2. Where are the hotel? _____
3. Can he to sing? _____
4. I don't can play tennis. _____
5. How much is these books? _____
6. She can swims very well. _____

Unit 7

It's Tom's!

1 Listen and practice.
🔊 19

Boy 1: Wow! Our tent is a mess! I can't find anything!
Boy 2: Yep.
Boy 1: Whose tennis racket is this?
Boy 2: Uh ... It's Diego's.
Boy 1: What about this cap?
Boy 2: It's Tom's, I think.
Boy 1: Whose boots are these?
Boy 2: They're Tom's ... or Diego's ...
Boy 1: What! ... What's a fish doing here?
Boy 2: Don't look at me!

| whose | ➡ | de quem |

SPEAKING

2 Listen and practice.

1. camera
2. key 
3. tennis racket 
4. umbrella 
5. boots 
6. dress 
7. pants 
8. jacket 

45

LESSON 1

3 **Look at the pictures and practice.**

Examples:
1. This is David's tennis racket.
2. These are Miriam's boots.

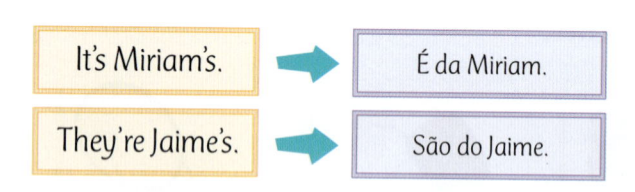

| It's Miriam's. | → | É da Miriam. |
| They're Jaime's. | → | São do Jaime. |

4 **Look at the pictures in Exercise 3 and practice the dialogs.**

Examples:
1. A: Whose tennis racket is this?
   B: It's David's.
   A: What color is it?
   B: It's white.

2. A: Whose boots are these?
   B: They're Miriam's.
   A: What color are they?
   B: They're black.

LESSON 2

WRITING

5 Look at the pictures. Answer the questions.

1. Teresa
2. Diego
3. Juan
4. Ana
5. Carla
6. Karen
7. Ray
8. Lucy

1. Whose dress is this?   *It is Teresa's.*
2. Whose shoes are these? _____
3. Whose tennis racket is this? _____
4. Whose umbrella is this? _____
5. Whose camera is this? _____
6. Whose pants are these? _____
7. Whose jacket is this? _____
8. Whose keys are these? _____

6 Fill in the blanks with *is*, *isn't*, *are*, or *aren't*.

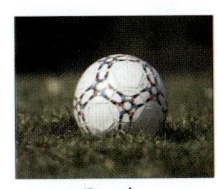

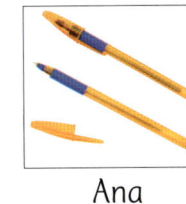

Paul   Ana   Ray   Linda

1. The book __isn't__ Ana's. It __is__ Ray's.
2. The ball _____ Linda's. It _____ Paul's.
3. The pens _____ Ana's. They _____ Linda's.
4. The notebook _____ Linda's. It _____ Paul's.

47

LESSON 2

LISTENING

7 Listen and number the pictures.

| A | B | C |
| D | E | F |

8 Listen again and fill in the chart about the items in Exercise 7.

	ITEM	COLOR	WHOSE IS IT? WHOSE ARE THEY?
A			
B			
C			
D			
E			
F			

LESSON 3

READING

9 Read the message. Then, match the items to the people.

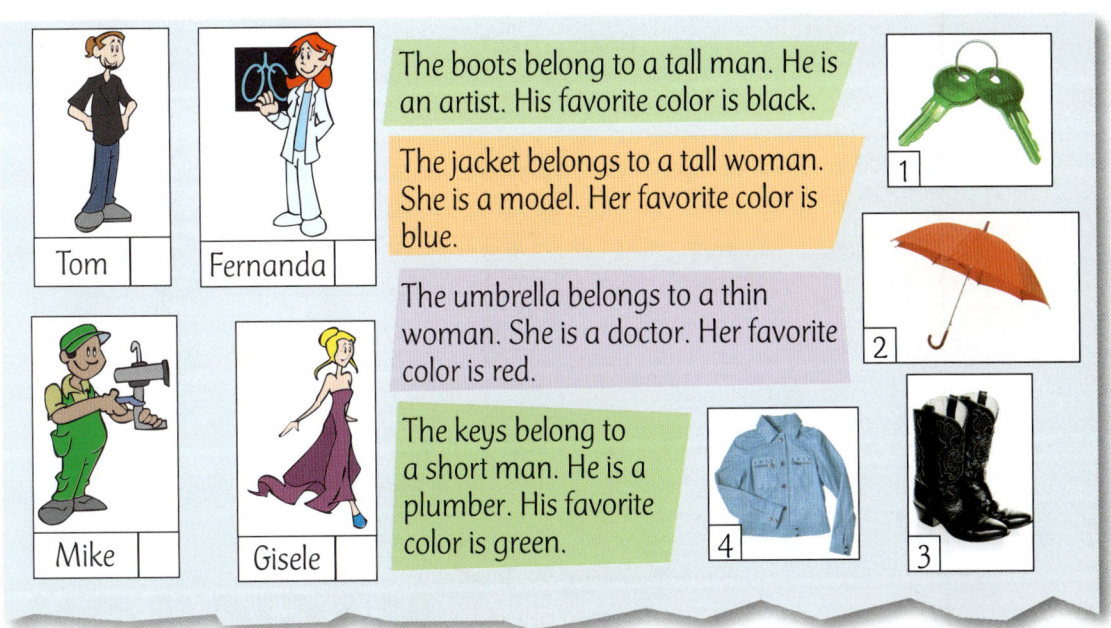

Tom

Fernanda

Mike

Gisele

The boots belong to a tall man. He is an artist. His favorite color is black.

The jacket belongs to a tall woman. She is a model. Her favorite color is blue.

The umbrella belongs to a thin woman. She is a doctor. Her favorite color is red.

The keys belong to a short man. He is a plumber. His favorite color is green.

1. (keys)
2. (umbrella)
3. (boots)
4. (jacket)

10 Complete the sentences about the items in Exercise 9.

The keys are (1) ___Mike's___ . The umbrella is (2) _____ . The boots are (3) _____ and the jacket is (4) _____ .

11 Answer the questions.

1. What is Tom's favorite color?   It is _____
2. Who is a doctor?   _____
3. Are the boots Fernanda's?   _____
4. Is the umbrella Gisele's?   _____
5. What is Mike's favorite color?   _____

GRAMMAR

POSSESSIVE (GENITIVE) CASE
Noun +**'s**:   Diego**'s** umbrella   Ana**'s** dress   Bob**'s** car

QUESTION WORD – Whose

Questions	Answers
Whose umbrella is this?	It is Ana**'s**.
Whose books are these?	They are Diego**'s**.

(See Grammar Reference, charts 6 and 13, pages 157 and 160.)

VOCABULARY

dress   umbrella
pants   keys
jacket   camera
boots   tennis racket
tent   anything
fish

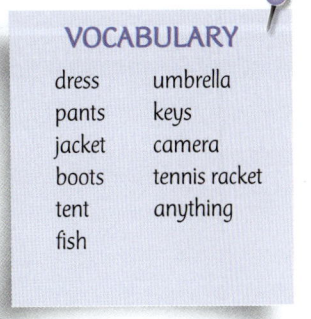

Pace Mix

NUMBER • 003 • JUNE

TONGUE TWISTER

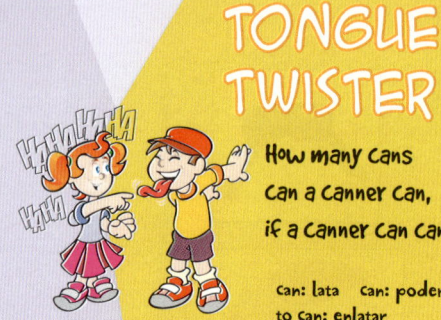

How many cans can a canner can, if a canner can can cans?

can: lata   can: poder
to can: enlatar
canner: enlatador

Whose dress is it?

Write the words and find the name.

next   ruler   artist   eraser   teacher   American

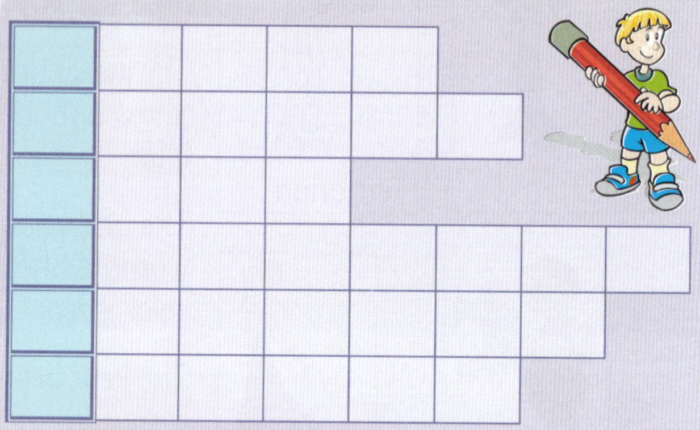

MAGIC BOX

I	soccer	the
not	can	he
girls	play	piano

Can you find more than 10 sentences in the box?

SUMMER CAMPS

Summer camp is a supervised program for children and/or teenagers (usually) during the summer months in some countries. Children and adolescents are "campers", and the adult supervisors are counselors.

Traditionally, a summer camp is a woodsy place with hiking, canoeing, and campfires.

The primary purpose of most camps is to create positive youth development.

camp: acampamento   children: crianças   teenager: adolescente   woodsy: localizado num bosque
hiking: caminhada   campfire: fogueira   youth: juventude   development: desenvolvimento

Unit 8

I'm studying.

1 Listen and practice.
🎧 22

Ann: What are you doing, Jeff?
Jeff: I'm studying.
Ann: What are you studying?
Jeff: I'm busy, Ann!
Ann: It looks like a drawing ...
Jeff: Go away, Ann!
Ann: What is it? Let me see ...
Oh, you're drawing the picture of a girl!
Jeff: Go away!
Mother: Jeff! Ann! What's going on?
Ann: Mom, Jeff's in love!
Jeff: Ann!

What are you doing? ➡ O que você está fazendo?

It looks like a drawing. ➡ Parece um desenho.

SPEAKING

2 Read and practice.

talk ➡ talk**ing**   eat ➡ eat**ing**   listen ➡ listen**ing**   drink ➡ drink**ing**

1. What's he doing?
   He's talking on the phone.

2. What are they doing?
   They're listening to the radio.

3. What are you doing?
   We're drinking milk.

51

LESSON 1

3 **Look at the picture and practice the dialogs.**

Examples:
1. A: What's Sandra doing?
   B: She's talking on the phone.
2. A: What are Carol and Ann doing?
   B: They're listening to the radio.

> eating   doing   drinking   listening   talking

4 **Look at the picture in Exercise 3. Tell a friend about the people.**

1. Pat / talk on the phone
   Pat is not talking on the phone.
2. Jack / draw a picture
   Jack is drawing a picture.
3. Meg and Kim / listen to the radio
4. Carol and Ann / watch TV
5. Will and Tom / talk
6. Mike / drink a milk shake
7. Will and Tom / eat sandwiches
8. Pat / play the guitar

LESSON 2

WRITING

5 **Write what the people are doing.**

1. What are you doing?
   (eat a banana)

   I'm eating a banana.

2. What's he doing?
   (wash the car)

   _____

3. What are they doing?
   (watch TV)

   _____

4. What's he doing?
   (cook)

   _____

5. What are you doing?
   (play the piano)

   _____

6. What is he doing?
   (do the dishes)

   _____

6 **Fill in the blanks. Use the correct form of do, listen, play, write, drink, or read.**

1. Are you ___doing___ your homework?   No, I _'m not._
2. Are they _____ to the radio?   Yes, they _____
3. Is she _____ orange juice?   No, she _____
4. Are you _____ soccer?   No, we _____
5. Is he _____ a magazine?   Yes, he _____
6. Are you _____ e-mails?   Yes, I _____

53

LESSON 2

LISTENING

7 Listen and number the pictures.

A B C

D E F

WRITING

8 Write sentences to describe the pictures in Exercise 7.

(wash) 1. <u>The girl is washing the car.</u>
(eat) 2. _____
(read) 3. _____
(watch) 4. _____
(talk) 5. _____
(wash) 6. _____

9 Write a similar dialog about a person in your house.

A: Is Jane studying?
B: No, she isn't.
A: What is she doing?
B: She is cooking.

LESSON 3

READING

10 **Read about a Charity Bazaar.**

Good morning. This is Fred Berry from B.C.C. I'm talking to you from Leicester School where kids are collecting articles for their Annual Charity Bazaar.

Cindy Lee, an 8th grader, is talking to us. She's responsible for the Bazaar.

Reporter: Cindy, are all the kids cooperating?

Cindy: Yes, everybody is helping: some students are collecting clothes. Some are walking around the neighborhood asking for gifts. Others are organizing everything. The teachers and parents are also helping.

Reporter: Congratulations, Cindy. Congratulations, Leicester School.

11 **Underline and correct the mistakes.**

1. Cindy Lee is a <u>reporter</u>. Cindy Lee is a student.
2. Fred Berry is responsible for the Bazaar. _____
3. Teachers are watching the students. _____
4. Leicester is the name of a soccer team. _____
5. Some students are washing clothes. _____
6. Some students are drawing gifts. _____
7. The parents are organizing everything. _____

GRAMMAR

PRESENT PROGRESSIVE TENSE

AFFIRMATIVE
I **am** walk**ing**.
You **are** walk**ing**.
He/She/It **is** walk**ing**.
We **are** walk**ing**.
They **are** walk**ing**.

NEGATIVE
I'**m** not walk**ing**.
You **aren't** walk**ing**.
He/She/It **isn't** walk**ing**.
We **aren't** walk**ing**.
They **aren't** walk**ing**.

QUESTIONS
Am I walk**ing**?
Are you walk**ing**?
Is he/she/it walk**ing**?
Are we walk**ing**?
Are they walk**ing**?

FORMING THE PRESENT PROGRESSIVE

talk – talk**ing**
write – writ**ing**
swim – swim**ming**

study – study**ing**
dance – danc**ing**
run – run**ning**

do – do**ing**
read – read**ing**

VOCABULARY

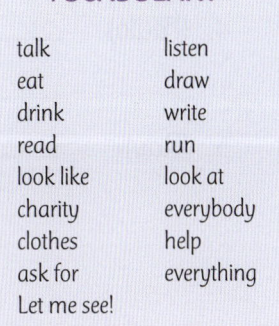

talk
eat
drink
read
look like
charity
clothes
ask for
Let me see!

listen
draw
write
run
look at
everybody
help
everything

(See Grammar Reference, chart 7, page 157.)

Review 7-8

1 **Unscramble the letters to form words.**

1. sesrd — **D**_ress_
2. yke — **K**_____
3. btoso — **B**_____
4. aertkc — **R**_____
5. ecrmaa — **C**_____
6. tnsap — **P**_____
7. ulbalmer — **U**_____
8. skcso — **S**_____
9. hsrost — **S**_____
10. obko — **B**_____

2 **Now use the words in Exercise 1 to write dialogs.**

1. (Melissa) A: _Whose dress is this?_
   B: _It's Melissa's._
2. (Jack) _____
3. (Linda) _____
4. (Paulo) _____
5. (Ray) _____
6. (Ben) _____
7. (Matt) _____
8. (Alice) _____
9. (Maggie) _____
10. (Ricardo) _____

3 Look at the house. Answer the questions.

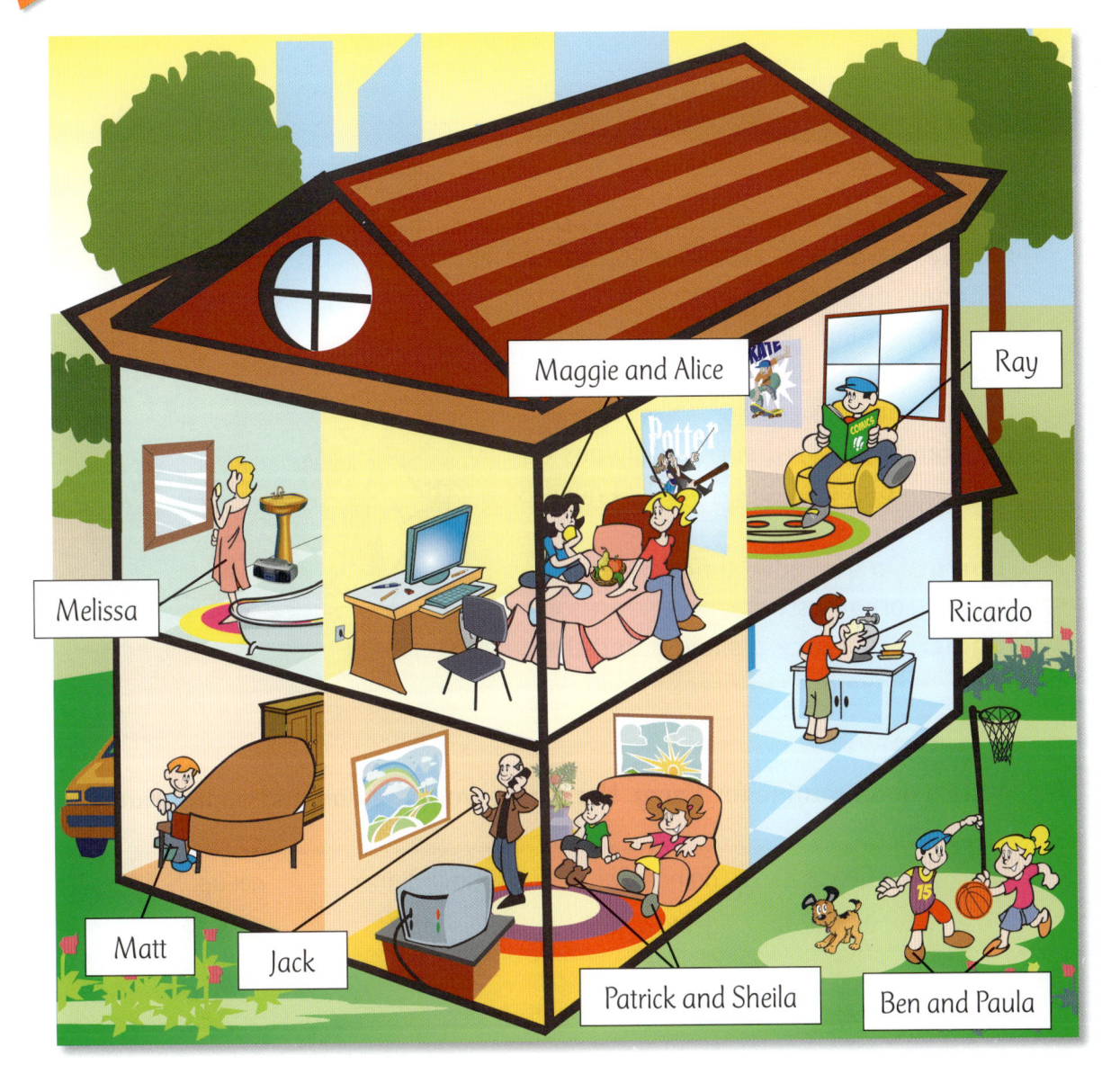

1. What is Ricardo doing? _He's washing the dishes._
2. What are Maggie and Alice doing? _____
3. What is Matt doing? _____
4. What is Ray doing? _____
5. What are Ben and Paula doing? _____
6. What is Jack doing? _____
7. What is Melissa doing? _____
8. What are Patrick and Sheila doing? _____

Project 2

HEALTH

Routines

1 Read the conversation.

Maggie: Hi, Larry! How are you doing?
Larry: I'm a little tired.
Maggie: Really? Why?
Larry: I go to bed late and get up at 5:45.
Maggie: That's very early. I always go to bed before 10:00. I need 8 hours sleep.
Larry: Do you have time for breakfast?
Maggie: Yes, I take a shower and then have a good breakfast.

2 Write a good routine for Larry. Use words from the box and appropriate times.

| go to bed | do homework | have dinner | ~~get up~~ |
| have breakfast | get to school | watch TV | get home |

1. 6:00
   get up
2. _____
3. _____
4. _____
5. _____
6. _____
7. _____
8. _____

Eating habits

3 Look at the examples of food below. Put them in the correct food group.

- ~~cake~~
- lasagna
- broccoli
- yogurt
- chicken
- carrot
- ice cream
- strawberry
- fish
- banana
- cheese
- macaroni
- lettuce
- turkey
- toast

FATS, OILS, AND SWEETS (a little)	DAIRY PRODUCTS (2 – 3 servings a day)	MEAT, EGGS, BEANS, AND NUTS (2 – 3 servings a day)	FRUIT (2 – 4 servings a day)	BREAD, CEREAL, PASTA, RICE (6 – 11 servings a day)
cake				

4 Can you complete the chart with more examples?

Project

Prepare a healthful menu for a day. Include food selections for breakfast, lunch and dinner. Use the information above. Show your menu to the class.

Unit 9

I like salad.

1 Listen and practice. 🎧 25

Julia: What do you want for lunch, kids?
Jerry: I like fast food. I want fries.
Julia: No way. Let's have real food. What do you want, Karen?
Karen: Hmm … I want salad, … and chicken. I like salad.
Jerry: Yuck!
Julia: How about you, Yan? Do you like chicken?
Yan: No. I like fish.
Jerry: Yuck!
Julia: Now you, Jerry. Do you want meat? Chicken?
Jerry: I don't. I want a hamburger!

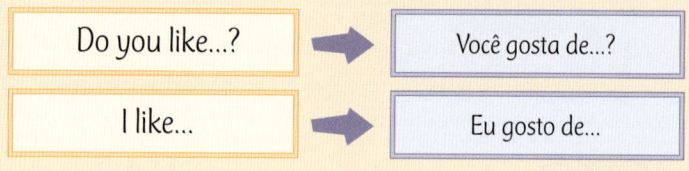

Do you like…? ➡ Você gosta de…?

I like… ➡ Eu gosto de…

SPEAKING

2 Listen and practice.

Do you like tacos?

Yes, I do.

No, I don't.

HOT DOG
FRENCH FRIES
HAMBURGER
SODA
TACO

60

LESSON 1

3 **Look at the pictures and practice the dialogs.**

Examples:
1. A: Do you like cereal?
   B: Yes, I do.
2. A: Do you like chicken?
   B: No, I don't.

BREAKFAST

1. toast
2. egg 
3. cereal 

LUNCH

4. soup
5. salad 
6. sandwich 

DINNER

7. rice
8. beans 
9. chicken 
10. fish 

DRINKS

11. milk
12. orange juice 
13. coffee 
14. milkshake

LESSON 2

4 Look at the pictures in Exercise 3. Practice the dialog.

Example:
A: What do you like for breakfast? (lunch) (dinner)
B: I like toast and milk.

WRITING

5 Write what the people like or don't like.

| I / You / We / They | like chicken. |
| I / You / We / They | don't like eggs. |

1. (they) _They like orange juice, but they don't like coffee._
2. (you) _____ 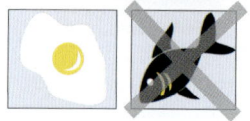
3. (I) _____ 
4. (we) _____ 
5. (they) _____ 
6. (I) _____ 
7. (we) _____ 
8. (you) _____

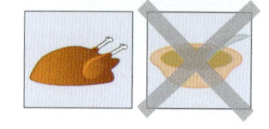

LESSON 2

LISTENING

6 Listen and fill in the chart. Use ✓ (= like) or ✗ (= don't like).

🔊 26

	CARLOS	JULIA
toast		
cereal		
eggs		
coffee		
soup		
salad		
rice		
beans		
chicken		
fish		
sandwiches		

WRITING

7 Write what you like for each meal.
1. (I / breakfast) _I like _____ for breakfast._
2. (I / lunch) _____
3. (I / dinner) _____

8 Write questions.
1. (you / beans / lunch) _Do you like beans for lunch?_
2. (they / soup / dinner) _____
3. (you / chicken / lunch) _____
4. (they / toast / breakfast) _____
5. (they / cereal / lunch) _____
6. (you / rice / dinner) _____
7. (you / salad / lunch) _____
8. (they / eggs / breakfast) _____

LESSON 3

READING

9 Read the menu and the order. Write the totals.

	KAREN	YAN	JERRY	JULIA
	salad	fish	hamburger	salad
	chicken	potatoes	potatoes	beef
	soda	ice cream	milkshake	coffee
Total				

MENU

salad .... $ 1.25   soda .... 25 c
chicken ...... $ 4.25   juice .... 80 c
beef .... $ 5.75   ice cream ..... 75 c
fish .... $ 6.50   coffee .... $ 2
potatoes .... $ 1.25
hamburger .... $ 3.75
milkshake .... $ 1.60

10 Look at the order. Write their answers.

1. Do you like soda, Karen? __Yes, I do.__
2. Jerry, do you like fish? _____
3. Do you like ice cream, Yan? _____
4. Do you like salad, Jerry? _____
5. Julia, do you like coffee? _____
6. Yan, do you like potatoes? _____
7. Do you like hamburgers, Julia? _____
8. Karen, do you like beef? _____

WRITING

11 Prepare a menu for one day of the week.

MONDAY   TUESDAY   WEDNESDAY   THURSDAY   FRIDAY   SATURDAY   SUNDAY

This is the MENU for …

GRAMMAR

SIMPLE PRESENT: LIKE – I / you / we / they

AFFIRMATIVE
I like fish.

NEGATIVE
I don't like fish.

Questions
Do you like fish?

What do you like for lunch?

Answers
Yes, I do.
No, I don't (do not).
I like fish for lunch.

(See Grammar Reference, charts 8 and 9, pages 158 and 159.)

VOCABULARY

hamburger   toast
taco   cereal
hot dog   French fries
fast food   soup
sandwich   salad
orange juice beans
milkshake   chicken
soda   fish
coffee   eggs
milk   rice

Pace Mix

NUMBER • 004 • AUGUST

TRADITIONAL RHYME

IT'S RAINING, IT'S POURING

It's raining, it's pouring;
The old man is snoring.
He went to bed and he
Bumped his head
And he couldn't get up in the morning.

to pour: chover forte
to go, went: ir, foi
to get up: levantar
to snore: roncar
bump: bater

Communication

What to say in a restaurant.

Waiter: Are you ready to order?
You: Yes. I'll have mashed potatoes, roast beef, and some salad.
Waiter: How do you want the beef? Rare, medium, or well-done?
You: Well-done.
Waiter: Anything to drink?
You: Just water, please.

I'll have: Vou querer
rare: malpassado
mashed potatoes: purê de batatas
well-done: bem passado

Crossword

What are they doing?

10. S I N G I N G

65

Unit 10

Stretch your arms!

1 Listen and practice. 🎵 27

- Good morning! I said, GOOD MORNING!
- Morning.
- OK, guys. Run around the yard for 2 minutes!
- OK, guys. Now, stretch! First, stretch your arms. Then stretch your hands. Now stretch your legs and feet.
- Touch your left ear with your right hand. Touch your right ear with your left hand.
- Very, good.
- Steve, what's the matter with you? Don't open your mouth. Open your eyes!
- You're sleepy today! Jump up and down to wake up.

| What's the matter with you ? ➡ O que há com você ? |

66

LESSON 1

SPEAKING

2 **Listen and practice.**

Example: Touch your ear.

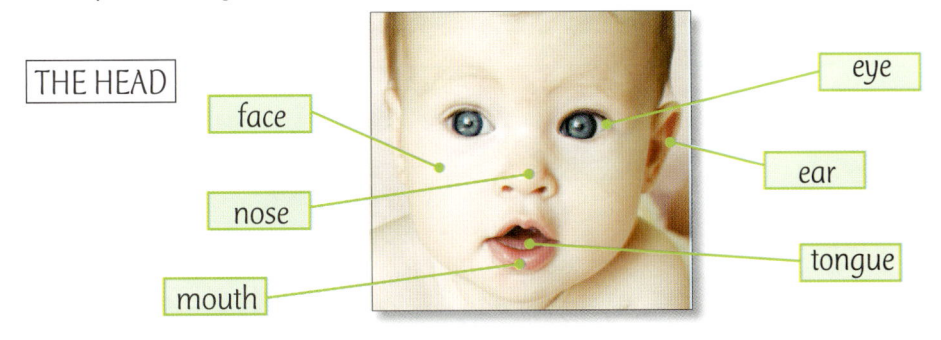

THE HEAD

- face
- nose
- mouth
- eye
- ear
- tongue

1. touch your ear
2. open your mouth
3. close your eyes
4. point to your nose
5. show your tongue
6. close your left eye

3 **Listen and practice.**

THE BODY

- head
- neck
- shoulder
- elbow
- arm
- hand
- leg
- knee

WRITING

4 **Write four commands. Then tell a friend what to do.**

Example: Touch your left leg.

67

LESSON 2

SPEAKING

5 **Read and practice.**

Example: A: Do you like Paul? B: Yes, I like him.
C: No, I don't like him.

1. Paul – him
2. Jeff – him 
3. Caroline – her 
4. Tom and Lucy – them 
5. Laura – her 
6. Ana and Liz – them 

WRITING

6 **Rewrite the sentences. Use *him*, *her*, or *them*.**

1. Call Mariana. _Call her._
2. Call Eduardo. _____
3. Call Max and Tina. _____
4. I like Hiroshi. _____
5. I don't like Jane. _____
6. I like Mary and Bob. _____
7. Look at Ana. _____
8. Look at José. _____
9. Look at Alice and Sue. _____
10. Don't look at Cathy. _____

LESSON 2

LISTENING

7 Listen and number.

| A | B | C |
| D | E | F |

READING

8 Read the directions and look at the map on page 70. Help Little Red Riding Hood find the places.

ROUTE 1

. Go straight ahead.
. Turn left at letter A.
. Go ahead.
. Turn right at letter B.
. Enter the village.
. Go to the 3rd house on the right.

That is the _____.

ROUTE 2

. Go straight ahead.
. Turn right at letter A.
. Go ahead.
. Turn left at letter B.
. Go ahead.
. Enter the village.
. Go to the 2nd house on the right.

That is _____'s house.

LESSON 3

9 Look at the map. Answer the questions.

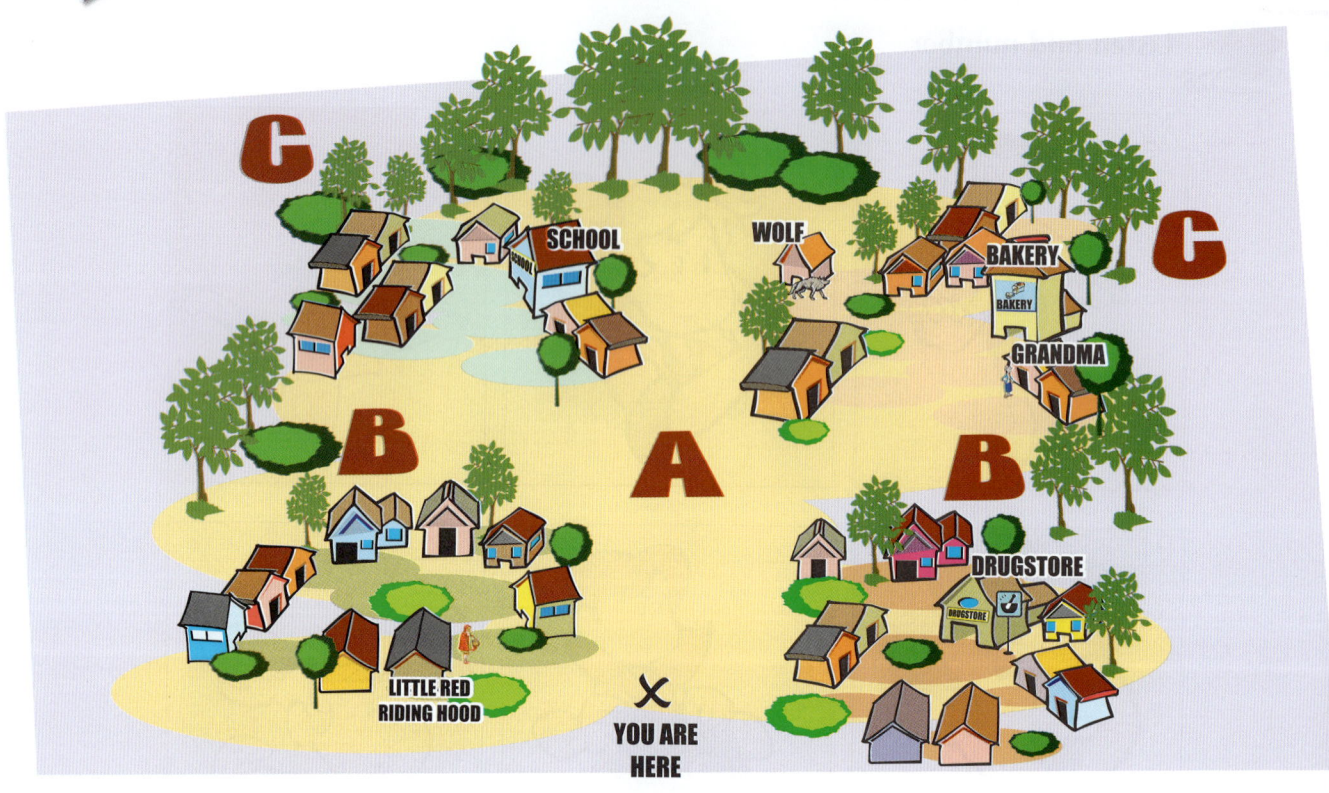

1. What is the best route to the wolf's house? _____
2. What is the best route to the bakery? _____
3. What is the best route to Little Red Riding Hood's house? _____
4. What is the best route to the drugstore? _____

WRITING

10 Draw a treasure map. Write instructions to find the treasure.

GRAMMAR

IMPERATIVES
Open your mouth.   **Don't open** your mouth.

PRONOUNS

SUBJECT	OBJECT	
She	her	**She** is sad. Call **her**.
He	him	**He** is angry. Don't look at **him**.
They	them	**They** are tired. Help **them**.

(See Grammar Reference, charts 4 and 10, pages 156 and 159.)

VOCABULARY

face	body	knee
ear	head	foot
mouth	neck	eye
shoulder	nose	arm
tongue	elbow	hand
leg	village	stretch
touch	point	jump
wake up	right	left

70

Review 9-10

1 Find ten words for food.

I	Y	S	N	A	E	G	G	S	W
R	I	C	E	L	J	K	I	P	H
L	C	E	K	A	A	N	M	C	N
T	S	F	C	S	U	E	I	Q	B
S	A	I	I	E	E	W	L	E	E
A	L	S	H	X	D	G	K	E	A
O	A	H	C	N	D	I	G	J	N
T	D	R	A	T	R	F	G	S	S
I	T	S	S	X	S	O	U	P	V
D	H	W	C	E	R	E	A	L	N

2 Write the parts of the body.

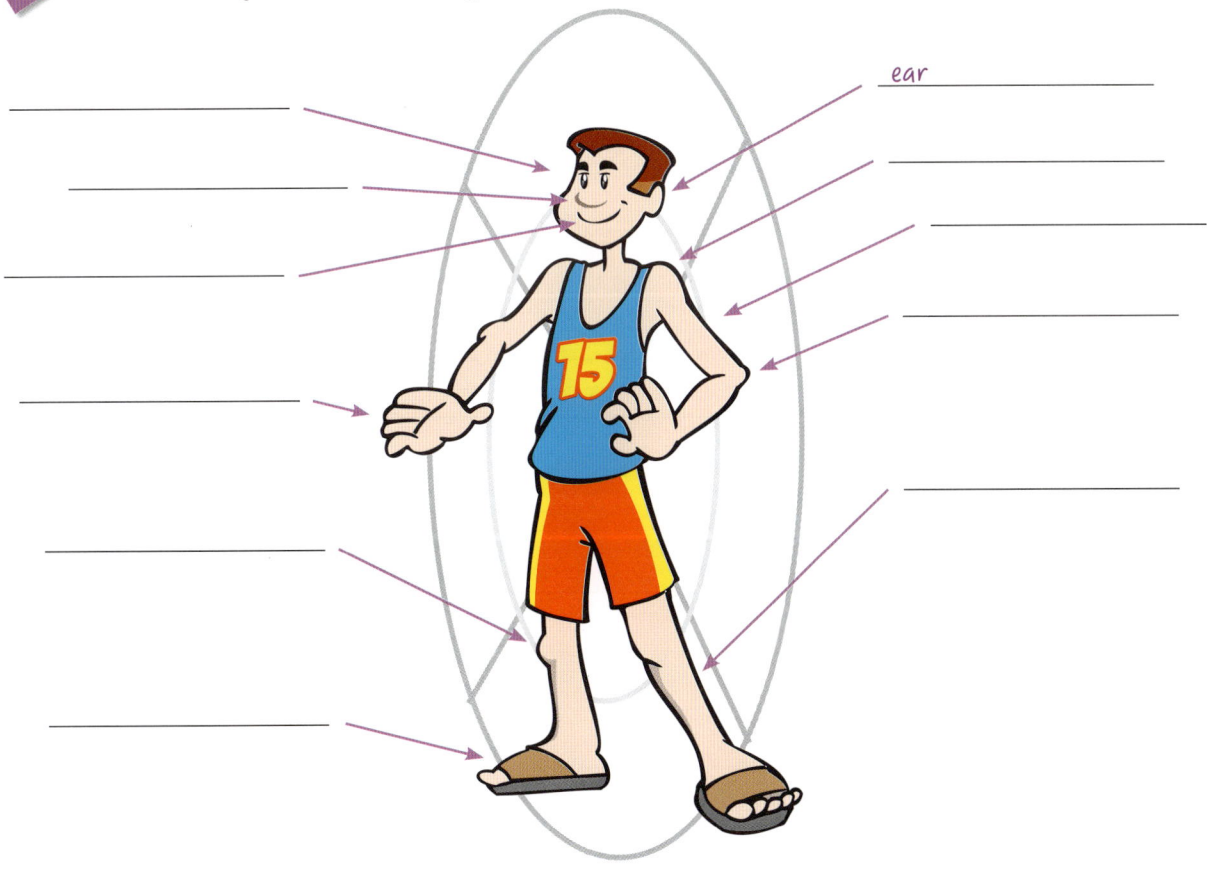

ear

3 **Rewrite these sentences. Use the correct pronoun.**

1. Call Tom. _Call him._
2. What's the matter with your sister? _____
3. Look at my girlfriend! _____
4. Don't call Jean and Sue. _____
5. I like your grandmother. _____
6. Look at Patricia. _____

4 **Match the questions with the answers.**

_e_ 1. How much is a soda?   a. No, they don't.
___ 2. Do you like chicken?   b. They're Carrie's.
___ 3. Whose socks are these?   c. He's very tired.
___ 4. Do they like tea?   d. It's David's.
___ 5. Are you hungry?   e. It's 99 cents.
___ 6. Whose notebook is this?   f. She likes pizza.
___ 7. What's the matter with Jim?   g. Yes, I do.
___ 8. What does your sister like?   h. No, I can't.
___ 9. Can you go out tonight?   i. At 1:30.
___ 10. What time does Bruce have lunch?   j. No, I'm not.

5 **Make these sentences negative.**

1. Open your mouth. _Don't open your mouth._
2. Point to your shoulder. _____
3. Close your eyes. _____
4. Move your foot. _____
5. Look at my tongue. _____
6. Point to my elbow. _____
7. Touch your toes. _____
8. Stretch your arms. _____
9. Touch your knees. _____
10. Open your eyes. _____

Unit 11

I run to school.

1 **Listen and practice.**
🔊 29

Boy: (yawning)
Girl: Sleepy?
Boy: Yeah. I get up at 7:00 every day.
Girl: Oh, come on! Seven o'clock is not that early!
Boy: Why? What time do you get up?
Girl: I get up at 6:00. What time do you get to school?
Boy: At 7:15.
Girl: 7:15! Do you walk to school?
Boy: No, I don't. Actually, I run to school.

SPEAKING

2 **Practice the dialog.**

Example:
A: What time do you get up?
B: I get up at 6 o' clock.

1. get up
2. have breakfast 
3. have lunch 
4. have dinner 

73

LESSON 1

3 **Look at the pictures and practice.**

Example: A: Do you have lunch at 12 o'clock?
B: Yes, I do.
C: No, I don't. I have lunch at 1 o'clock.

1. get up
2. wash your face 
3. brush your teeth 
4. leave home 
5. catch a bus 
6. get to school 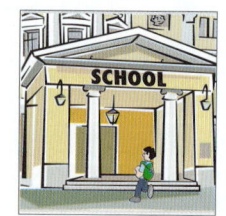
7. get home 
8. have dinner 
9. go to bed 

WRITING

4 **Answer the questions about yourself.**

1. What time do you wash your face?
   _____

2. Do you have breakfast at 1 o'clock?
   _____

3. Do you get to school at 7 o'clock?
   _____

4. What time do you leave school?
   _____

5. What time do you have lunch?
   _____

6. Do you have dinner at 8 o'clock?
   _____

7. What time do you go to bed?
   _____

LESSON 2

5 Write about the twin sisters, Amanda and Samantha.

> we get up — 7:30
> we have breakfast — 8:30
> we leave home — 9:00
> we get to school — 9:15
> we have lunch — 12:35
> we get home — 4:00
> we have dinner — 5:30
> we go to bed — 10:00

1. get up / 7:30 — They get up at 7:30.
2. have breakfast / 8:00 — They don't have breakfast at 8:00.
3. leave home / 9:00 _____
4. get to school / 9:15 _____
5. have lunch / 13:00 _____
6. get home / 4:00 _____
7. have dinner / 5:30 _____
8. go to bed / 10:30 _____

LISTENING

6 Listen and number the pictures.
🎧 30

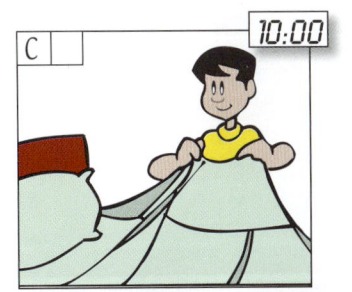

A — 9:00
B — 8:00
C — 10:00
D — 11:00
E — 7:00
F — 9:00

75

LESSON 2

READING

7 Read about these triplets' life.
🎧 31

We Like Being Triplets

Hi. My name is Shaun. I am a triplet. I have two sisters, Carol and Jill.

We like being triplets because we can all be in the same grade at school and play together at recess.

We get up at the same time, 6:10. We have a big breakfast with Mom and Dad.

We leave home at 6:55 and wait for the school bus in front of our house. We come back at 4:00 with Mom.

We have lunch at school. There, my sisters have their friends and I have mine.

My sisters share a bedroom and sometimes they share clothes. We like to play together a lot. There is always somebody to talk to and there is always someone to play with.

Sometimes I don't like being a triplet 'cause when I don't want to do what the others want to, they start to argue with me.

I like to run track and play soccer. When I grow up, I want to be a zoo keeper. I like to talk to my mom, just the two of us.

When I tell a new friend that I am a triplet, she thinks it is cool!

But, in fact, we are no different from any other family.

LESSON 3

8 **Circle the correct alternative.**

1. Carol is Shaun's [sister. / brother.]

2. They leave home [at the same time. / at different times.]

3. They go to school [by car. / by bus.]

4. They come back home at [6:55. / 4:00.]

5. Shaun's sisters share [a bedroom. / breakfast.]

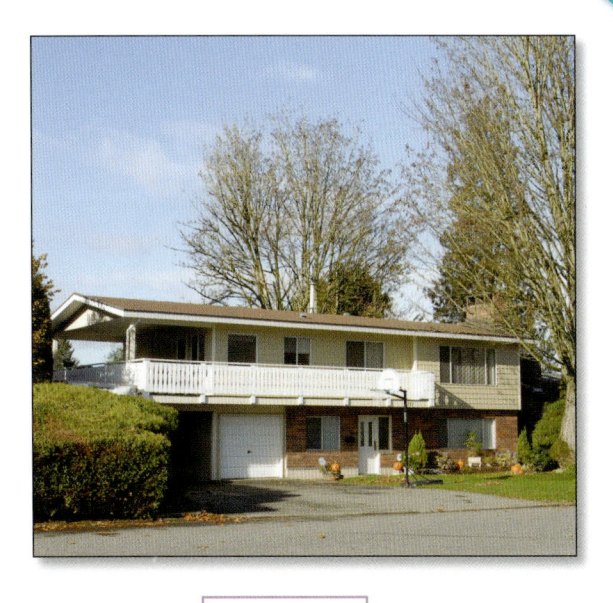

6. The triplets [share / don't share] clothes.

9 **Answer the questions.**

1. How many brothers do the girls have? _____
2. What time do the triplets get up? _____
3. Where do they have lunch? _____
4. Do the girls share clothes? _____
5. What do they like? _____

WRITING

10 **Describe your routine. Use:** *get up, brush, wash, have, leave,* **etc.**

I get up at …

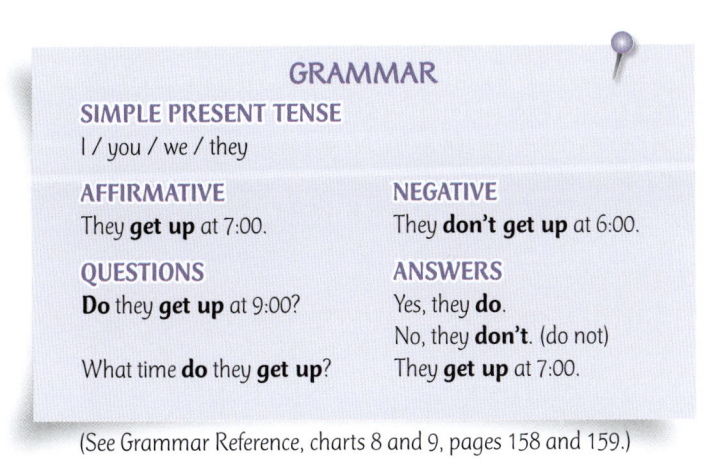

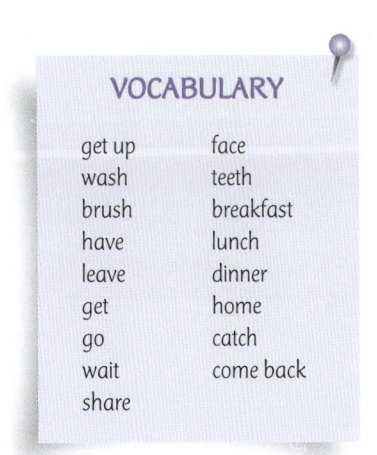

GRAMMAR

SIMPLE PRESENT TENSE
I / you / we / they

AFFIRMATIVE
They **get up** at 7:00.

NEGATIVE
They **don't get up** at 6:00.

QUESTIONS
Do they **get up** at 9:00?

ANSWERS
Yes, they **do**.
No, they **don't**. (do not)

What time **do** they **get up**?
They **get up** at 7:00.

(See Grammar Reference, charts 8 and 9, pages 158 and 159.)

VOCABULARY

get up	face
wash	teeth
brush	breakfast
have	lunch
leave	dinner
get	home
go	catch
wait	come back
share	

Pace Mix

NUMBER • 005 • SEPTEMBER

TONGUE TWISTER

If you understand
If you understand, say "understand".
If you don't understand, say "don't understand".
But if you understand and say "don't understand".
How do I understand that you understand? Understand!

to understand: entender   to say: dizer   how: como

WORD BOX

Connect the letters to find 8 words.

H	A	N
R	D	E
M	L	G
K	O	U
N	E	T
Y	H	E

The most frequent questions to twins

1. Are you guys really twins?
2. What is your favorite color?
3. Do you spend a lot of time together?
4. Do you pretend to be each other?
5. What are your favorite numbers?
6. How many people are in your family?
7. What color are your eyes?
8. What type of music do you listen to?
9. What sports do you guys play?
10. What do you do for fun?

fun: diversão

World News

Triplets become doctors

Sydney triplets become doctors at a ceremony at the University of New South Wales on Friday 10, December. This is the first recorded instance of triplets graduating together as medical practitioners in the world.

"We generally end up doing the same thing," said one of the triplets. " It is more of a coincidence that we like the same things."

"We try not to broadcast that we are triplets," said Martina.

The triplets share a part-time job, a car and even a mobile phone.

to become: tornar-se   instance: exemplo   to graduate: graduar-se   together: juntos   to end up: terminar   to broadcast: difundir

Unit 12

He studies every day.

1 Listen and practice.
🎧 32

Coordinator: I'm a bit worried about Sean.
Father: Me too. His grades aren't very good.
Coordinator: Yes. He has many Cs and Ds.
Father: Does he come to classes every day?
Coordinator: Yes, he does. He never misses a class.
Father: Does he do his homework?
Coordinator: Yes, he does.
Does he study for the tests?
Father: Yes, he studies every day …
Coordinator: Does he turn the TV off?
Father: Hmm … No, he doesn't.
Coordinator: Maybe that's the problem.

SPEAKING

2 Read and practice.

I write e-mails.

He writes e-mails.

I study English.

He studies English.

I go to the bank.

She goes to the bank.

I watch TV.

He watches TV.

79

LESSON 1

3 **Look at the pictures and practice the dialogs.**

Examples:

1. A: Does he read the newspaper?
   B: Yes, he does.

2. A: Does she write e-mails?
   B: No, she doesn't.

1.  read the newspaper
2.  write e-mails
3.  play the flute
4.  watch TV
5.  study Spanish
6.  play tennis
7.  go to school
8.  clean his room

4 **Look at the schedules and practice the dialogs.**

Example: A: What does Mom do on Monday?
B: She plays tennis.

Mom

Monday	play tennis
Tuesday	go to the supermarket
Wednesday	cook dinner
Thursday	study Spanish
Friday	go to the supermarket

Jim

Sunday	wash the car
Monday	clean room
Wednesday	clean room
Friday	play soccer

LESSON 2

LISTENING

5 Look at the schedules in Exercise 4. Listen and check True or False.

🎵 33

	1	2	3	4	5	6	7	8
True								
False								

6 Listen and number the pictures.

🎵 34

A — 9:30
B — 8:30
C — 10:00
D — 8:00
E — 5:00
F — 2:00

WRITING

7 Write about the pictures in Exercise 6.

1. (have)   _She has breakfast_ _____ at 8:00.
2. (brush) _____ at 8:30.
3. (read)   _____ at 10:00.
4. (clean) _____ at 2:00.
5. (play)   _____ at 5:00.
6. (watch) _____ at 9:30.

LESSON 2

READING

8 Read about Alezeta, a girl from Burkina-Faso.

At about 5:30am, 13-year-old Alezeta wakes up in a poor, 'quartier' of Ouagadougou, Burkina-Faso, and begins her long and tiring day.

She collects firewood piled up on one side of the house. Then she builds a fire to heat water. She prepares a basic morning meal for her parents, brothers, and sisters.

Next, she helps to bathe her younger brothers and sisters from a bucket of water. After that, she dresses the children for school.

When they leave, Alezeta begins her list of household chores. She cleans the house, washes the cooking pots, washes the clothes, hangs them out to dry, goes to the market to buy food, and collects water at the water pump. She works till the end of the day.

By 8:30 or 9:00pm, she crawls onto the thin mattress that she shares with her sister.

Alezeta is just another girl from Burkina – Faso.

9 Correct the information.
1. The girl doesn't live in a poor area. *The girl lives in a poor area.*
2. Her day is calm. _____
3. Her parents prepare the morning meal. _____
4. She has brothers only. _____
5. They use a bucket of water to clean the house. _____
6. She collects water at the market. _____
7. She sleeps on a big bed. _____

LESSON 3

10 **Answer the questions.**

1. How old is Alezeta?
   She is 13 years old.

2. Where does she live?
   _____

3. What time does she get up?
   _____

4. Does she live in a modern house?
   _____

5. Why does she build a fire in the morning?
   _____

6. In your opinion, is it possible to find a similar situation in your country?
   _____

WRITING

11 **Write about your family's routine. Use *get up, brush, wash, have, leave*, etc.**

My mother gets up at 6 in the morning.

GRAMMAR

SIMPLE PRESENT TENSE
He / She / It

AFFIRMATIVE	NEGATIVE
He cook**s**.	He **doesn't cook**.

QUESTION	ANSWERS
Does he **cook**?	Yes, he **does**.
	No, he **doesn't** (does not).

SPELLING
1. play – play**s**   read – read**s**   speak – speak**s**   dance – dance**s**
   (regular plural)
2. kiss – kiss**es**   wash – wash**es**   watch – watch**es**   go – go**es**
   (verbs ending in **-ss, -sh, -ch, -o**)
3. study – stud**ies**   (verbs ending in **-y** preceded by one consonant)

(See Grammar Reference, charts 2, 8, and 9, pages 155 and 158.)

VOCABULARY

read	newspaper
do	letter
cook	flute
write	room
study	watch
maybe	wash
clean	go
run	love
worried about	begin
wake up	prepare
build	

Review 11-12

1 Look at the chart and answer the questions.

	SUNDAY	MONDAY	TUESDAY	WEDNESDAY	THURSDAY	FRIDAY	SATURDAY
morning		(cooking)			(tennis)		(writing)
afternoon	(washing)		(watching TV)	(golf)		(baseball)	
evening		(washing dishes)			(reading)		(brushing teeth)

1. What does she do on Thursday morning?
   She plays tennis.
2. What does she do on Sunday afternoon?
   _____
3. What does she do on Wednesday afternoon?
   _____
4. What does he do on Saturday evening?
   _____
5. What does she do on Thursday evening?
   _____

2 Look at the chart and write questions for the answers.

1. _What does she do on Monday morning?_ She cooks.
2. _____ He brushes his teeth.
3. _____ She plays tennis.
4. _____ He washes the dishes.
5. _____ She reads a book.

3 Write questions for the answers.

1. <u>Does she have green eyes?</u>
   Yes, she does.

2. _____
   No, he doesn't. He has long hair.

3. _____
   No, I don't. I prefer hamburgers.

4. _____
   Yes, I do. I have a very big dog.

5. _____
   No, she doesn't. She lives in Recife.

6. _____
   No, he doesn't. He speaks English and Portuguese.

7. _____
   Yes, she does. She cleans her room every Saturday.

8. _____
   No, I don't. I go to school at seven o'clock.

4 Combine the two sentences. Follow the example.

1. My dog's eyes are brown.
   My dog has large eyes.
   <u>My dog has large brown eyes.</u>

2. My dog's tail is brown.
   My dog has a short tail.
   _____

3. My cat's eyes are blue.
   My cat has beautiful eyes.
   _____

4. My dog's teeth are white.
   My dog has small teeth.
   _____

5. My dog's legs are white.
   My dog has long legs.
   _____

6. My bird's beak is yellow.
   My bird has a strong beak.
   _____

Project 3

MULTICULTURALISM

My class team

1 Interview your classmates. Write the name of someone in your class who can...

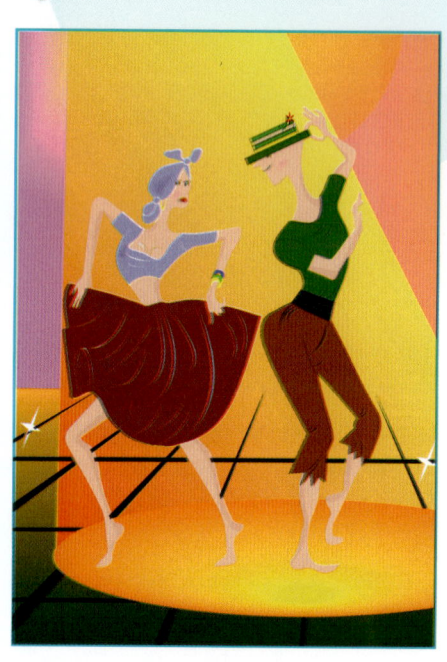

1. dance samba very well _____
2. speak Spanish _____
3. play the guitar _____
4. play soccer very well _____
5. use a computer well _____
6. cook _____
7. sing very well _____
8. swim _____
9. play the piano _____
10. speak English very well _____

Project

1. Interview your family.
2. What can they do very well? What can't they do very well?
3. Present the results to the class.

An international family.

2 **Read about Angelina Jolie.**

Angelina Jolie is a very famous American actress. She is a beautiful woman and she works a lot. She likes to participate in different movies (comedies, romance, action movies), but she helps the United Nations, too. She always visits countries with difficulties (Cambodia, Sierra Leone, Tanzania, and Kenya) and she talks about the problems in these areas. She goes to refugee camps and talks to important people about possible solutions. Angelina wants to change the world.

She is married to Brad Pitt. He is a very popular American movie star, too. Sometimes he travels with Angelina. They have six children: three adopted children, a biological daughter (Shiloh) and twins (Vivienne and Knox).

3 **Answer the questions.**

1. Where is Angelina Jolie from? _____
2. What is her job? _____
3. How does she help the UN? _____
4. How many children does she have? _____
5. Do you know any celebrities that help the world? What do they do to help?
_____

Project

1. Choose a celebrity that does something to help.
2. Find out more about what they do to help.
3. Present the results to the class.

Unit 13

He has long ears!

1 Listen and practice.
🔊 36

Girl: Samson! Samson!
Boy: Looking for your dog?
Girl: Yeah.
Boy: What does it look like?
Girl: He's a small, brown dog. He has short legs and long ears. He's just a puppy.
Boy: I'm looking for my dog, too. It's a 'she'. Her name's Moon.
Girl: What does she look like?
Boy: She's big, white, and has a long tail.
Girl: Oh, here they come.
Boy: Great! I guess Samson has a new friend!

SPEAKING

2 **Read and practice.**
Examples:

1. A: Do you have a pet?
   B: Yes, I do. I have a pet fish.

2. A: Does she have a pet?
   B: Yes, she does. She has a frog.

LESSON 1

3 Listen and practice.

1. beak
2. feet 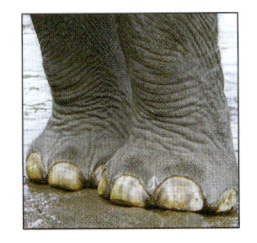
3. legs 
4. ears 
5. horns 
6. tail 
7. shell 
8. teeth 
9. neck 
10. wings 

4 Play with a friend.

Example:
A: Does it have long legs?
B: No, it doesn't.
A: Does it have wings?
B: Yes, it does.
A: Does it have a large beak?
B: Yes, it does.
A: Is it a toucan?
B: Yes, it is.

giraffe
toucan 
beaver
flamingo
antelope
turtle
crab 
rabbit
bear 
alligator 

89

LESSON 2

LISTENING

5 Listen and number the pictures.
🎵 37

| A | B | C |
| D | E | F |

WRITING

6 Write about the animals. Use opposites in the sentences.
1. (giraffes / necks) _Giraffes don't have short necks. They have long necks._
2. (alligators / teeth) _____
3. (turtles / legs) _____
4. (antelopes / ears) _____
5. (toucans / beaks) _____
6. (horses / tails) _____

7 Describe.
a flamingo - _____
a rabbit - _____
a bear - _____
a turtle - _____

90

LESSON 2

READING

8 Read these reports about some endangered species.

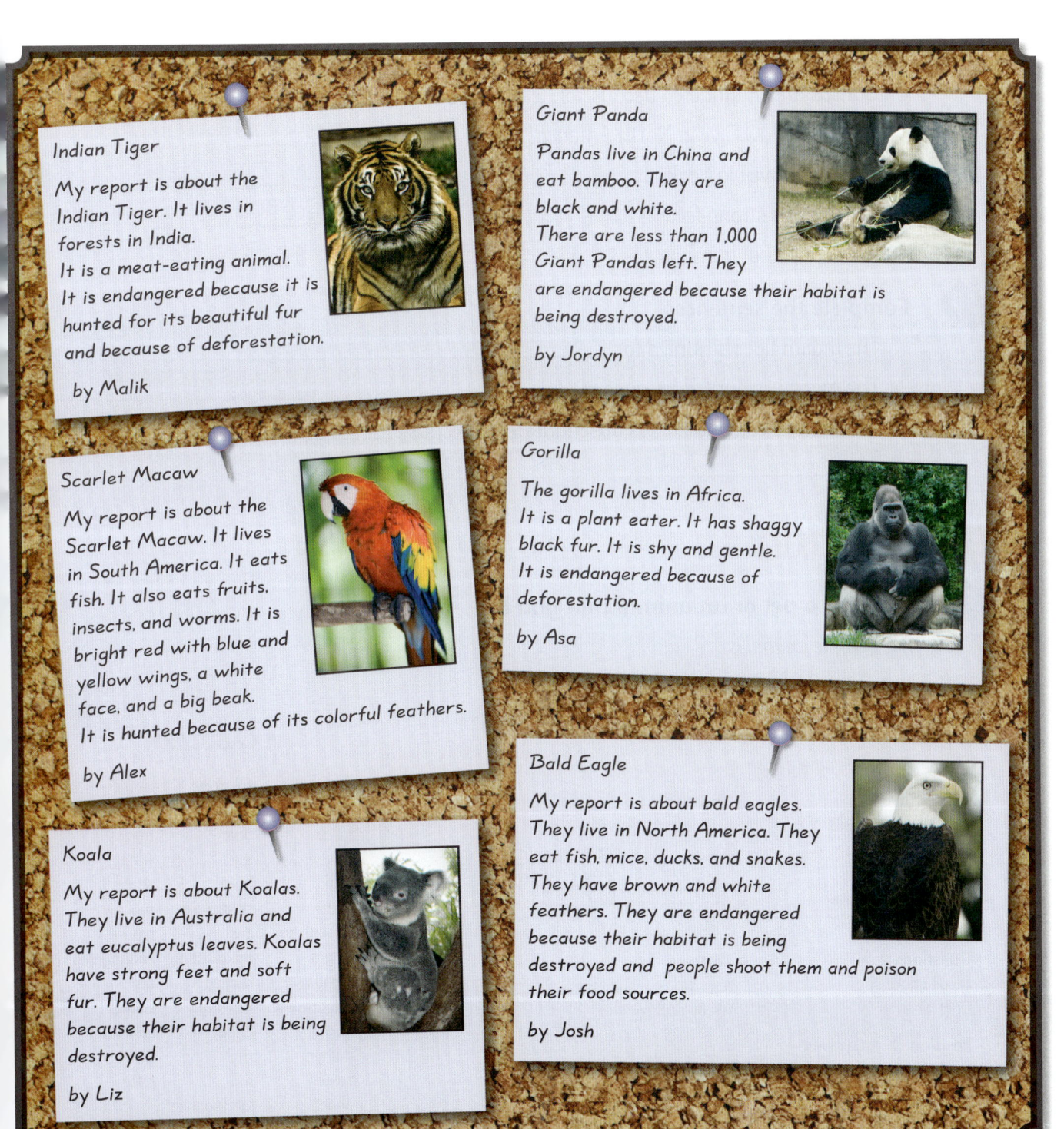

Indian Tiger

My report is about the Indian Tiger. It lives in forests in India.
It is a meat-eating animal. It is endangered because it is hunted for its beautiful fur and because of deforestation.

by Malik

Giant Panda

Pandas live in China and eat bamboo. They are black and white.
There are less than 1,000 Giant Pandas left. They are endangered because their habitat is being destroyed.

by Jordyn

Scarlet Macaw

My report is about the Scarlet Macaw. It lives in South America. It eats fish. It also eats fruits, insects, and worms. It is bright red with blue and yellow wings, a white face, and a big beak. It is hunted because of its colorful feathers.

by Alex

Gorilla

The gorilla lives in Africa. It is a plant eater. It has shaggy black fur. It is shy and gentle. It is endangered because of deforestation.

by Asa

Koala

My report is about Koalas. They live in Australia and eat eucalyptus leaves. Koalas have strong feet and soft fur. They are endangered because their habitat is being destroyed.

by Liz

Bald Eagle

My report is about bald eagles. They live in North America. They eat fish, mice, ducks, and snakes. They have brown and white feathers. They are endangered because their habitat is being destroyed and people shoot them and poison their food sources.

by Josh

LESSON 3

9 **Check True or False.**

	True	False
1. Indian tigers live in Africa.	___	✓
2. Pandas are black and brown.	___	___
3. Indian tigers eat meat.	___	___
4. Gorillas are endangered because of deforestation.	___	___
5. Scarlet macaws live in North America.	___	___
6. Macaws have big beaks.	___	___
7. A koala has strong feet.	___	___
8. Bald eagles eat bamboo.	___	___

10 **Complete the sentences.**

1. The Indian tiger is hunted for _____.
2. The macaw is hunted because of _____.
3. Pandas, gorillas and koalas are endangered because _____
_____.

WRITING

11 **Describe a pet or an animal that you like.**

My favorite animal is . . .

GRAMMAR

Simple Present – have

Affirmative
I	have
You	have
He/She/It	has
We	have
They	have

Negative
I	don't
You	don't
He/She/It	doesn't	have…
We	don't
They	don't

Questions
Do you have…?
Does he have…?

Answers
Yes, I do.
Yes, he does.

Position Of Adjectives
Size before color
large brown ears   long pink legs

VOCABULARY

flamingo	antelope	beaver
rabbit	alligator	crab
turtle	tiger	frog
pet	tail	wing
beak	horn	shell
teeth	bald eagle	macaw
poison	live	report
forests	meat-eating	endangered
because	hunted	fur
deforestation	less than	snakes
worms	bright	colorful
feathers	shy	gentle
leaves	soft	mice
shoot	food sources	

(See Grammar Reference, charts 8 and 12, pages 158 and 159.)

Pace Mix

NUMBER • 006 • OCTOBER

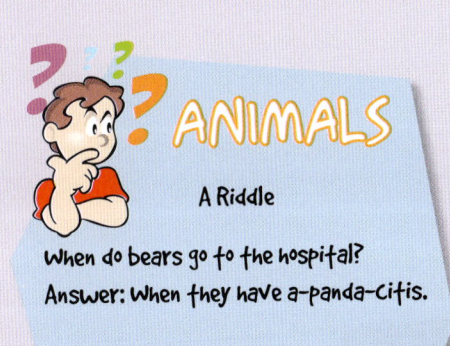

ANIMALS

A Riddle
When do bears go to the hospital?
Answer: When they have a-panda-citis.

riddle: charada

A Question

Which animals are more similar to humans: cats or dogs?
Answer: Cats.
Dogs can be our best friends, but cats and humans use identical parts of the brain to process emotions.

AN ACTION

Find out what Joe does in the evening.

1. One, ... , three.
2. I ... the newspaper.
3. They ... letters.
4. It's 2 o'...
5. He ... the dog.
6. We play ... .
7. I don't like ... .
   I like math.
8. Friday, ... , Sunday.
9. I live on 27 Maple ...

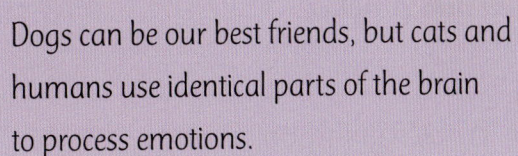

RECIPE

Peach Freeze

serves: 3

Ingredients:

1/2 c. milk

1 c. sliced peaches

1 tsp. sugar

Directions:

• Put the milk into an ice cube tray and freeze until solid.

• Put the "milk cubes" into the blender.

• Then put the peaches and sugar into the blender.

• Blend until everything is all mixed together and very smooth.

• Serve right away.

Nutritional analysis (per serving): 65 calories; 2 g protein; 15 g carbohydrate; 1 mg cholesterol; 25 mg sodium; 53 mg calcium; 0.3 mg iron

c. (cup): xícara   tsp. (teaspoon): colher de chá   sliced: fatiado
ice cube tray: forma de gelo   to freeze: congelar   blender: liquidificador
mixed: misturado   smooth: homogêneo   right away: imediatamente

Unit 14

They never help!

1 Listen and practice. 🔊 39

Husband: What's going on, Gloria?
Wife: I don't know. Why?
Husband: Well, Ana is setting the table. She always watches TV at this time of the day.
Wife: How strange! Look at Teresa ... She's cooking! I can't believe it.
Husband: She usually reads in the afternoon, right?
Wife: Yeah! Oh, no! Juan and Diego are doing the dishes.
Husband: They never do the dishes!
Wife: They never help in the kitchen. What's going on?
Children: Happy Anniversary, Mom and Dad!!!

always ➡ sempre   usually ➡ geralmente

SPEAKING

2 Listen and practice.

1. set the table
2. make the bed 
3. take out the garbage 
4. do the dishes 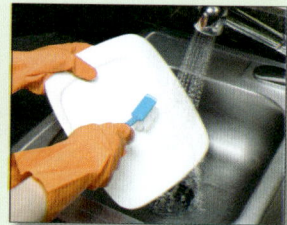

94

LESSON 1

3 **Fill in the chart with *always*, *usually*, or *never*. Ask each other questions about your routines.**

Example: A: Do you ever make your bed?
B: Yes. I usually make my bed.
C: No. I never make my bed.

| ever | → | alguma vez |
| never | → | nunca |

1. make my bed
2. clean my room
3. do the dishes
4. set the table
5. take out the garbage
6. cook lunch
7. read a magazine
8. play soccer
9. surf the Net
10. watch TV

1. usually
2. _____
3. _____
4. _____
5. _____
6. _____
7. _____
8. _____
9. _____
10. _____

LESSON 2

LISTENING

4 Listen and write Y (yes) or N (no).

🔊 40

	Clean the room	Do the dishes	Wash the car	Set the table	Cook dinner	Make the bed
Nick						Y
Mary						
Diego						
Cathy						
Bob						
Ana						

WRITING

5 Now write about the people in Exercise 4.

1. (Nick) _Nick makes the bed._
2. (Mary) _____
3. (Diego) _____
4. (Cathy) _____
5. (Bob) _____
6. (Ana) _____

6 Match the parts of the dialogs.

1. Is she reading?
2. Do you play tennis?
3. What are they doing?
4. What does he like?

a. They're cooking dinner.
b. He likes hamburgers.
c. No, she's cleaning the room.
d. No, I don't.

LESSON 2

READING

7 Read about the dogs' adoption party.
🎵 41

Mateus Stein is a fifteen-year old boy from Blumenau. He adopts and takes care of stray dogs. There are over 25 dogs of all breeds and sizes in his house right now.

His sister, Patricia, always helps him. She washes the dogs, takes them to the vet, and finds new homes for some of the animals.

Every year, they celebrate the Dog Adoption Day. Mateus invites his friends and their pets. He serves snacks for the kids and bones for the dogs. The dogs usually get lots of presents: toys, balls, and even dog clothes.

The dogs are having a nice Adoption Day Party. Some dogs are peacefully eating their bones. Others are playing. But a very small dog, Fido, is running after a cat.

8 Underline the mistakes and correct the sentences

1. Mateus adopts <u>big cats</u>.   *Mateus adopts stray dogs.*
2. Mateus doesn't have a sister.   _____
3. The boy takes the dogs to the vet.   _____
4. They celebrate the dogs' birthdays.   _____
5. Fido is a large dog.   _____
6. The dogs never get many presents.   _____
7. Some dogs are eating snacks.   _____
8. Fido is eating a bone.   _____

97

LESSON 3

9 **Answer the questions.**

1. How old is Mateus? _He is 15._
2. Who helps him? _____
3. Does his sister wash the dogs? _____
4. Who does he invite to the party? _____
5. What is Fido doing? _____
6. Do you have a pet? Do you look after it? _____

WRITING

10 **Look at the pictures and answer the questions. Use the words given.**

1. always / wash the car
   What does she always do on Sundays?
   She always washes the car.

2. watch TV / now
   What are you doing now?
   _____

3. play tennis / now
   What is she doing now?
   _____

4. usually / write letters
   What do you usually do in the morning?
   _____

GRAMMAR

FREQUENCY ADVERBS

always	I **always** go to school in the morning.
usually	I **usually** have cereal for breakfast.
never	I **never** get up at 10:00.
ever	Do you **ever** do the dishes?

WE USE THE SIMPLE PRESENT
when something is always true: Bob lives in Lubbock, Texas.
when talking about routines: I always eat breakfast.

WE USE THE PRESENT PROGRESSIVE
when we talk about now: Teresa is cooking dinner.

VOCABULARY

believe	size
stray	vet
breeds	peacefully
bone	snack
invite	
set the table	
make the bed	
take out the garbage	
do the dishes	
take care of	

(See Grammar Reference, chart 11, page 159.)

Review 13-14

1. Look at the chart and write about Meggin's routine.

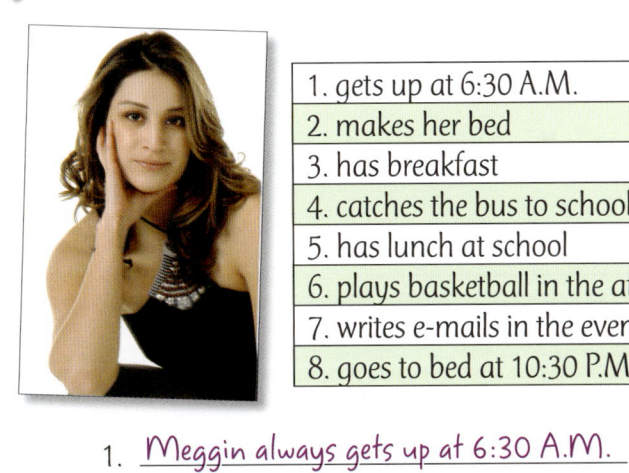

	ALWAYS	USUALLY	NEVER
1. gets up at 6:30 A.M.	✓		
2. makes her bed			✓
3. has breakfast		✓	
4. catches the bus to school	✓		
5. has lunch at school		✓	
6. plays basketball in the afternoon			✓
7. writes e-mails in the evening		✓	
8. goes to bed at 10:30 P.M.	✓		

1. Meggin always gets up at 6:30 A.M.
2. _____
3. _____
4. _____
5. _____
6. _____
7. _____
8. _____

2. Answer the questions.

1. What are you doing now?
   _____

2. What is your best friend doing now?
   _____

3. What time do you have lunch?
   _____

4. When do you play volleyball?
   _____

5. What time does your mother / father get up?
   _____

3 **Complete the sentences with *have* or *has*.**

1. My dog ____has____ large black eyes.
2. Hamburgers _____ many calories.
3. Does she _____ a pet?
4. Alligators _____ sharp teeth.
5. Do flamingos _____ short legs?

4 **Answer the questions. Use *always, usually* or *never*.**

1. When does your mother set the table?
   My mother always sets the table.
2. When does your cousin watch TV?
   _____
3. When do you make your bed?
   _____
4. When does your best friend write e-mails?
   _____
5. When does your English teacher read a book?
   _____
6. When do you do your English homework?
   _____

5 **Fill in the blanks with the correct form of the verb.**

1. It's 8 o'clock. I _'m having_ my breakfast. (have)
2. I usually __have__ cereal for breakfast. (have)
3. She always _____ TV on Saturday night. (watch)
4. She _____ TV now. (watch)
5. They usually _____ basketball on Saturday. (play)
6. They _____ basketball now. (play)
7. I _____ a letter now. (write)
8. You never _____ the dishes. (do)

Unit 15

I'm going to grandma's.

1 **Listen and practice.**
🎧 42

Rick: Where are you going for Thanksgiving, Julie?
Julie: We're going to grandma's in San Diego.
Rick: When are you going?
Julie: On Friday. Maria, my Italian friend, is coming too.
Rick: Cool. Is she happy?
Julie: Sure. It's her first Thanksgiving, you know.
Rick: Are you going by car?
Julie: No, we're going by bus, this time. What about you, Rick?
Rick: We're going to my uncle's in New York.
Julie: How are you going?
Rick: Probably by plane.

Where are you going? →	Para onde você vai?
How are you going? →	Como você vai?
When are you going? →	Quando você vai?

LESSON 1

SPEAKING

2 Look at the pictures and practice the dialog.

Example:

A: How are you going?

B: I'm going by car.

car   bus   plane   train   boat

3 Listen and practice.

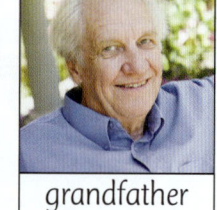

grandmother   grandfather   uncle   aunt   cousin

4 Practice the dialog.

Example:

A: Where's Camila going?

B: She's going to her cousin's house.

A: How is she going?

B: She's going by car.

A: When is she going?

B: She's going on Saturday.

ON

MONDAY TUESDAY WEDNESDAY THURSDAY FRIDAY SATURDAY SUNDAY

IN

JANUARY FEBRUARY MARCH APRIL MAY JUNE JULY AUGUST SEPTEMBER OCTOBER NOVEMBER DECEMBER

LESSON 2

LISTENING

5 Listen and number.

WHO	WHERE	HOW	WHEN	WITH
( ) Alex	( ) beach	( ) plane	( ) Tuesday	( ) cousin
( ) Tom	(1) mountains	( ) car	( ) Sunday	( ) aunt
( ) Cindy	( ) movies	( ) bus	( ) Wednesday	( ) uncle
( ) Carol	( ) shopping mall	( ) train	( ) Friday	( ) grandma
(1) Bob	( ) concert	( ) boat	( ) Saturday	( ) grandpa

WRITING

6 Write about two people from Exercise 5.

Tom is going to the shopping mall by car, on Tuesday, with his grandpa.

1. _____
2. _____

7 Look at the pictures and write where the people are going.

1. I / mountains   2. we / beach   3. they / shopping mall

1. _I am going to the mountains_____.
2. _____.
3. _____.

103

LESSON 2

READING

8 Read about Thanksgiving.

Thanksgiving is celebrated on the second Monday in October, in Canada. In the USA, Thanksgiving is celebrated on the fourth Thursday in November. It is one of the most important American holidays.

At Thanksgiving, Americans remember the first Pilgrims and give thanks for what they have. There are large parades across the country. Children wear costumes of turkeys, Pilgrims or Native American Indians. Families get together and celebrate with a large meal. They usually have turkey, mashed potatoes, cranberry sauce, sweet potatoes, corn, and pumpkin pie.

At Thanksgiving, you see thousands of people in airports or bus stations. They are all traveling to other cities and states to visit their relatives.

9 Complete the sentences.

1. Thanksgiving is celebrated in the _USA and Canada._
2. It is an important American _____.
3. On this day, people give thanks _____.
4. Families _____.
5. Americans celebrate it on the fourth _____.

LESSON 3

10 **Answer the questions.**

1. What do children wear?

   Children wear costumes.

2. How do families celebrate?

   _____

3. Do they usually eat turkey?

   _____

4. What do people usually do at Thanksgiving?

   _____

WRITING

11 **Read the e-card. Write a similar note. Say where you are going.**

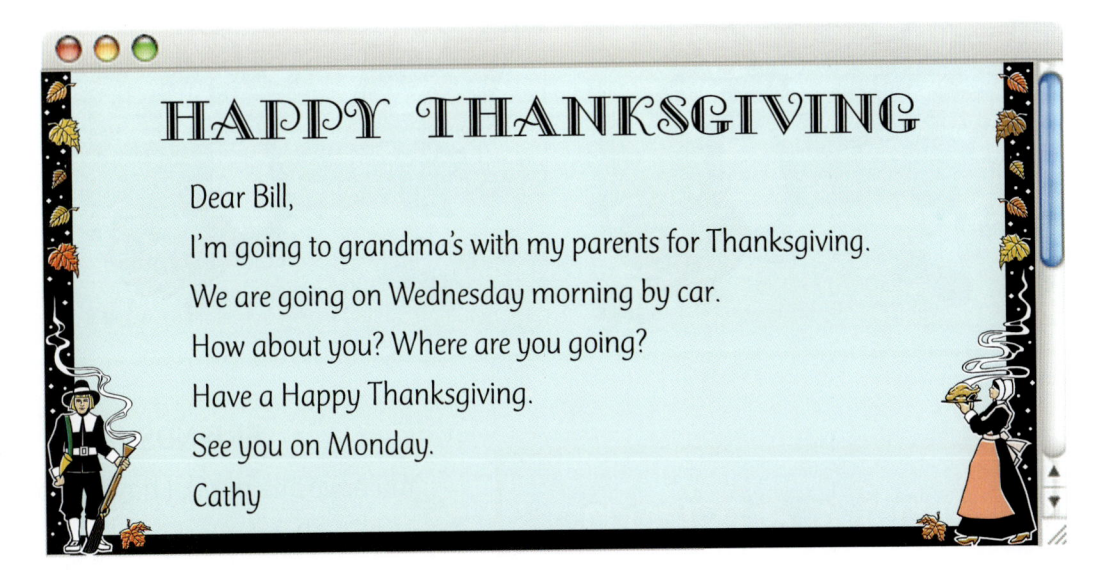

HAPPY THANKSGIVING

Dear Bill,

I'm going to grandma's with my parents for Thanksgiving.

We are going on Wednesday morning by car.

How about you? Where are you going?

Have a Happy Thanksgiving.

See you on Monday.

Cathy

GRAMMAR
REVIEW: QUESTION WORDS

Questions	Answers
Where are you going?	I'm going to the beach.
How are you going?	I'm going by car.
When are you going?	I'm going on Monday.

(See Grammar Reference, chart 13, page 160.)

VOCABULARY

train	grandfather
plane	grandmother
beach	aunt
mountains	uncle
movies	cousin
shopping mall	turkey
pumpkin pie	mashed potatoes
Thanksgiving	costume
wear	meal

105

Pace Mix

NUMBER • 007 • NOVEMBER

BIRDS

The Turkey

The turkey is native to northern Mexico and the eastern United States.

The male turkey is called a Tom. It is bigger and has more colorful plumage. The female is called a Hen.

- Domesticated turkeys cannot fly. Wild turkeys can fly for short distances.
- Turkeys sometimes spend the night in trees.
- Turkeys can have heart attacks.

northern: do norte (adj.)   eastern: do leste (adj.)   male: macho   female: fêmea   bigger: maior   wild: selvagem   to spend: passar   heart: coração

ATTENTION

Find 8 differences

Communication

What to say in a store

Salesperson: Hi, can I help you?
You: No, thanks. I'm just looking.
Salesperson: All right. If you need any help, just let me know. My name is Greg.
You: Sure. Thanks.

just: apenas   need: precisar

FRIENDS

A POEM

You have one hand, I have the other.
Put them together,
We have each other.
You help me,
And I'll help you
And together
We will see it through.
Across the land
Across the sea
Friends forever
We will always be.

Unit 16

I'm looking for a present.

1 Listen and practice.
45

Jim: Hi, Tony. What's up? Where are you going?
Tony: I'm going to the post office to pick up a letter.
Jim: Pick up a letter?
Tony: Yes! I'm taking part in Operation Santa Claus. You see, poor children send letters to Santa Claus asking for presents. Then volunteers take the letters, buy the presents, and send them to the kids.
Jim: Wow! That's cool!
Tony: How about you, Jim? What are you doing?
Jim: I'm looking for a present for my cousin, but I don't know what to give her.
Tony: Why don't you give her a CD?
Jim: That's a good idea. Thanks!

SPEAKING

2 Listen and practice.

Example:
A: What are you doing?
B: I'm looking for a Christmas present for my cousin.
A: Why don't you give him a T-shirt?
B: That's a good idea.

T-shirt    belt    sweater
book    pen

LESSON 1

3 **Look at the picture and practice the dialog.**

Example:

A: I'm looking for a Christmas present for my mom.

B: How much money do you have?

A: Not much.

B: Why don't you give her those shoes?

A: They are too expensive.

WRITING

4 **Look at the picture in Exercise 3 and write how much things cost.**

1. (camera) <u>The camera is fifty-two dollars and ninety-eight cents.</u>
2. (perfume) _____
3. (sandals) _____
4. (watch) _____
5. (blouse) _____
6. (skirt) _____
7. (bag) _____
8. (glasses) _____

LESSON 2

SPEAKING

5 **Practice the dialog.**

Example:
A: Where are you going for Christmas?
B: I'm going to Boston.
A: Do you go there every year?
B: No. We usually go to New York.

WRITING

6 **Write about where people go.**

1. she / usually / Miami / holidays – aunt
   <u>She usually goes to Miami on the holidays. Her aunts lives there</u>.

2. they / always / New York / Christmas – cousin
   _____.

3. we / usually / Toronto / Thanksgiving – brothers
   _____.

4. he / always / Chicago / Easter – grandmother
   _____.

5. I / usually / Bahia / Carnival – sister
   _____.

LISTENING

7 **Listen to the conversation and check True or False.**
46

	True	False
1. She's going to the mountains.	____	____
2. She's going by car.	____	____
3. She's going on Thursday.	____	____
4. She's coming back on Friday.	____	____
5. She's going with her brother, George.	____	____

LESSON 2

READING

8 Read the e-mail about Christmas holidays.

From: Anna
To: Laura
Subject: Christmas in London

Dear Laura,

How is everything?

Guess where I'm going for Christmas this year? To London!

As you know, I usually spend Xmas in New York, at my uncle's. I love NY in December with the decorated streets and the large Christmas tree at Rockefeller Center. But this time, we're going to grandpa's. Isn't that great?

Why don't you come, too?

London lights up at Christmas.

Grandpa usually goes to Trafalgar Square to see the traditional Christmas tree and listen to carols. We can ice skate at the Tower of London Ice Rink. We can also go to the West End and visit the big stores on Oxford Street and Regent Street.

The city is empty on Christmas Eve because the workers leave to visit their families across the country.

Think about it, OK?

Yours,

Anna

LESSON 3

9 **Circle the correct alternative.**

1. ⟨Laura / Anna⟩ usually spends Christmas ⟨in New York. / at home.⟩
2. The streets ⟨are / aren't⟩ decorated for Xmas in NY.
3. ⟨Anna / Laura⟩ is inviting ⟨Laura / Carol⟩ for Xmas.
4. On Christmas Eve, the workers ⟨go to / leave⟩ London.
5. The workers want to ⟨visit their families. / cross the country.⟩

10 **Answer the questions.**

1. Who is Anna going to visit for Xmas?
   She is going to visit her grandpa.
2. Where is there a large Christmas tree in NY?
   _____
3. Where does Anna's grandfather live?
   _____
4. What is there in Trafalgar Square?
   _____
5. In your opinion, is there great consumerism at Christmas time?
   _____

WRITING

11 **Think about the place you usually go to on a holiday. Say what you do there.**

I usually go to … I play …

GRAMMAR

REVIEW: Present Progressive

Questions	Answers
What are you doing?	I'm looking for a present.
Where are you going?	I'm going to Miami for Christmas.

REVIEW: Simple Present

Where does he live?	He lives in New York City.
Do you go there every year?	No. We usually go to Denver.

(See Grammar Reference, chart 7, page 157.)

VOCABULARY

present	skate
tie	belt
blouse	teddy bear
post office	look for
give	Why don't you?

Review 15-16

1 Look at the pictures. Write sentences. Use one means of transportation and one place.

1.  Chicago — bus
2. 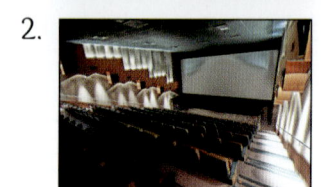 movies — taxi
3.  shopping mall — car
4.  Rio de Janeiro — plane
5.  beach — train
6.  mountains — boat

1. (He)   _He's going to Chicago by bus._
2. (She) _____
3. (We)   _____
4. (They) _____
5. (I)   _____
6. (She) _____

2 Look at the pictures and write the conversations.

1. (father)
A: I'm looking for a present for my father.
B: Why don't you give him a belt?

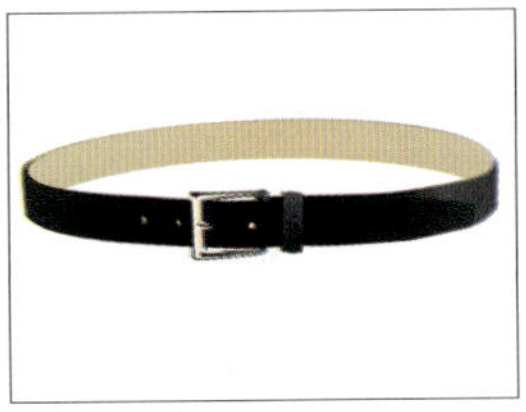

2. (uncle)
A: _____
B: _____

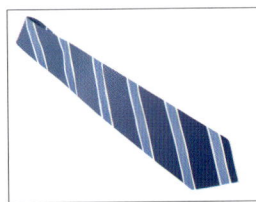

3. (sister)
A: _____
B: _____

4. (best friend)
A: _____
B: _____

5. (mother)
A: _____
B: _____

3 Complete the questions with *How, Where, Who, Why* or *When*.

1. _____ are you going to New York? I'm going by plane.
2. _____ are they going to London? They're going on Sunday.
3. _____ don't you give her a watch? It's too expensive.
4. _____ is going to Salvador with you? My sister.
5. _____ is she going? She's going to Madrid.

113

Project 4
ETHICS

Ethics and Values

Ethics is the study of human actions. It discusses what is "right and wrong" and what is in between. Ethics talks about "good behavior" and the personal qualities that are important for everyone to have.

1 **Read the sentences about Kate's family. Do you think their actions are RIGHT or WRONG?**

1. Kate helps her mother. She cooks dinner and cleans her bedroom. _____
2. Kate's father always throws paper on the street. _____
3. Kate's brother usually listens to very loud music at night. _____
4. Kate's cousin copies Kate's homework. _____
5. Kate's grandmother always tells the truth. _____

2 **Write three good actions that you usually do at home.**

I always help my father. I do the dishes and wash the car.

1. _____
2. _____
3. _____

Project

1. In small groups, make a list of "good behavior".
2. Choose the top ten and illustrate them. You can make a collage.
3. Present your poster to the class.
4. Vote and choose the best one.

Helping my community

3 **What do they do to help their community? Match the sentences with the pictures.**

- I always give up my seat to elderly people or pregnant women.
- I plant flowers in a community garden.
- I clean the beach every Saturday morning.
- I help blind people cross the street.
- I visit an orphanage and read to the kids.
- I paint the public hospital.

4 **What do you do to help your community?**

Project

Work in groups. Find an example of a problem in your community. Think about how you can help. Prepare a poster and present your suggestions to the class.

Project ACE 2

WORKBOOK

EDUARDO AMOS & ELISABETH PRESCHER

WITH VINICIUS NOBRE

PEARSON
Longman

UNIT 1

1 Find the plural of ten words.

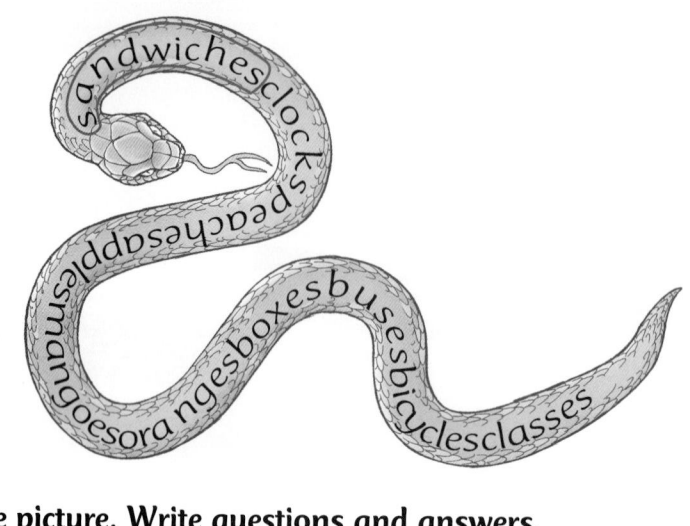

sandwiches, clocks, peaches, apples, mangoes, oranges, boxes, buses, bicycles, classes

2 Look at the picture. Write questions and answers.

1. (apples)   A: <u>How many apples are there?</u>
   B: <u>There are three apples.</u>

2. (sodas)   A: _____
   B: _____

3. (bananas)   A: _____
   B: _____

4. (sandwiches)   A: _____
   B: _____

5. (oranges)   A: _____
   B: _____

3 Read about Green Park. Answer the questions.

Green Park is near my school. It's my favorite place but it isn't large. There is a small lake in Green Park. It is called Mirror Lake. There is a large tree near it. There are many ducks on the lake and there are small boats, too. There is a picnic area near the lake. There are four picnic tables there. I love Green Park!

1. Where's Green Park?
   Green Park is near my school.
2. Is Green Park small?
   _____
3. How many picnic tables are there in the park?
   _____
4. How many lakes are there in the park?
   _____
5. Where is the picnic area?
   _____
6. Where is the large tree?
   _____

4 Answer the questions about yourself.
1. How many students are there in your class? _____
2. How many girls are there in your class? _____
3. How many doors are there in your classroom? _____
4. How many windows are there in your classroom? _____
5. How many books are there in your bag? _____

UNIT 2

1. Complete the text with *is* or *are*.

This is Mark's room. There _____ a bed and a desk. There _____ one chair. There _____ a computer on his desk. There _____ two calculators on his desk, too. There _____ four books under his desk. There _____ a shirt on his bed and there _____ three magazines under the chair. There _____ six shoes under his bed.

2. Read the text again and draw Mark's room.

3. Answer the questions.
1. Is there a bank near your house? _No, there isn't._
2. Is there a clock in your classroom? _____
3. Are there good restaurants near your school? _____
4. Are there many boys in your class? _____
5. Is there an eraser in your bag? _____
6. Are there computers in your school? _____
7. Is there a newsstand near your house? _____
8. Are there any books under your chair? _____

4 **Look at the picture and write about Beth's room. Use the words below.**

| computer   sofa   books   watch   dress |

This is Beth's room. There is a beautiful bed in her bedroom.
_____
_____
_____
_____
_____

5 **Describe your room.**
_____
_____
_____
_____
_____
_____

UNIT 3

1. Match the columns.

_h_ 1. a penny
___ 2. a nickel
___ 3. a dime
___ 4. a quarter
___ 5. half-a-dollar
___ 6. a dime and two nickels
___ 7. three quarters and a penny
___ 8. half-a-dollar and four dimes
___ 9. ten quarters
___ 10. six nickels

a. twenty cents
b. two dollars and fifty cents
c. thirty cents
d. twenty-five cents
e. fifty cents
f. ten cents
g. ninety cents
h. one cent
i. seventy-six cents
j. five cents

2. Complete the dialog with sentences from the box.

> Here is your change.
> How much is this cap?
> How much is it altogether?
> Here you are.
> It's fifty-two dollars and ninety-nine cents.
> ~~Can I help you?~~
> How much are those glasses?

A: _Can I help you?_

B: Yes, please. How much is this watch?

A: _____

B: _____

A: They're thirty-three dollars.

B: _____

A: It's only nine dollars and thirty-five cents.

A: Is that all?

B: Yes, _____

A: Let's see… That's forty-two dollars and five cents.

B: _____

A: Thank you very much. _____

3 Find the plural of the words in the box.

G	G	I	B	S	B	V	D	L	Y	N	O
A	H	Y	Z	A	U	M	G	E	B	P	U
D	S	Y	B	S	T	S	H	I	R	T	S
D	S	Y	H	T	S	T	N	P	S	S	J
R	R	R	S	O	E	S	E	S	U	B	U
E	A	Q	K	S	I	A	E	R	Z	K	U
S	L	W	I	J	N	W	Z	M	I	K	Z
S	L	Q	R	Z	N	V	E	O	W	E	G
E	O	F	T	V	E	H	A	K	S	B	S
S	D	O	S	X	P	P	Q	H	B	Z	B
B	P	E	W	A	T	C	H	E	S	Q	Q
S	S	E	I	T	R	A	P	H	Q	J	U

- ~~battery~~
- party
- address
- skirt
- top
- penny
- dollar
- watch
- T-shirt
- bus

4 Look at the pictures and write the dialogs. Follow the example.

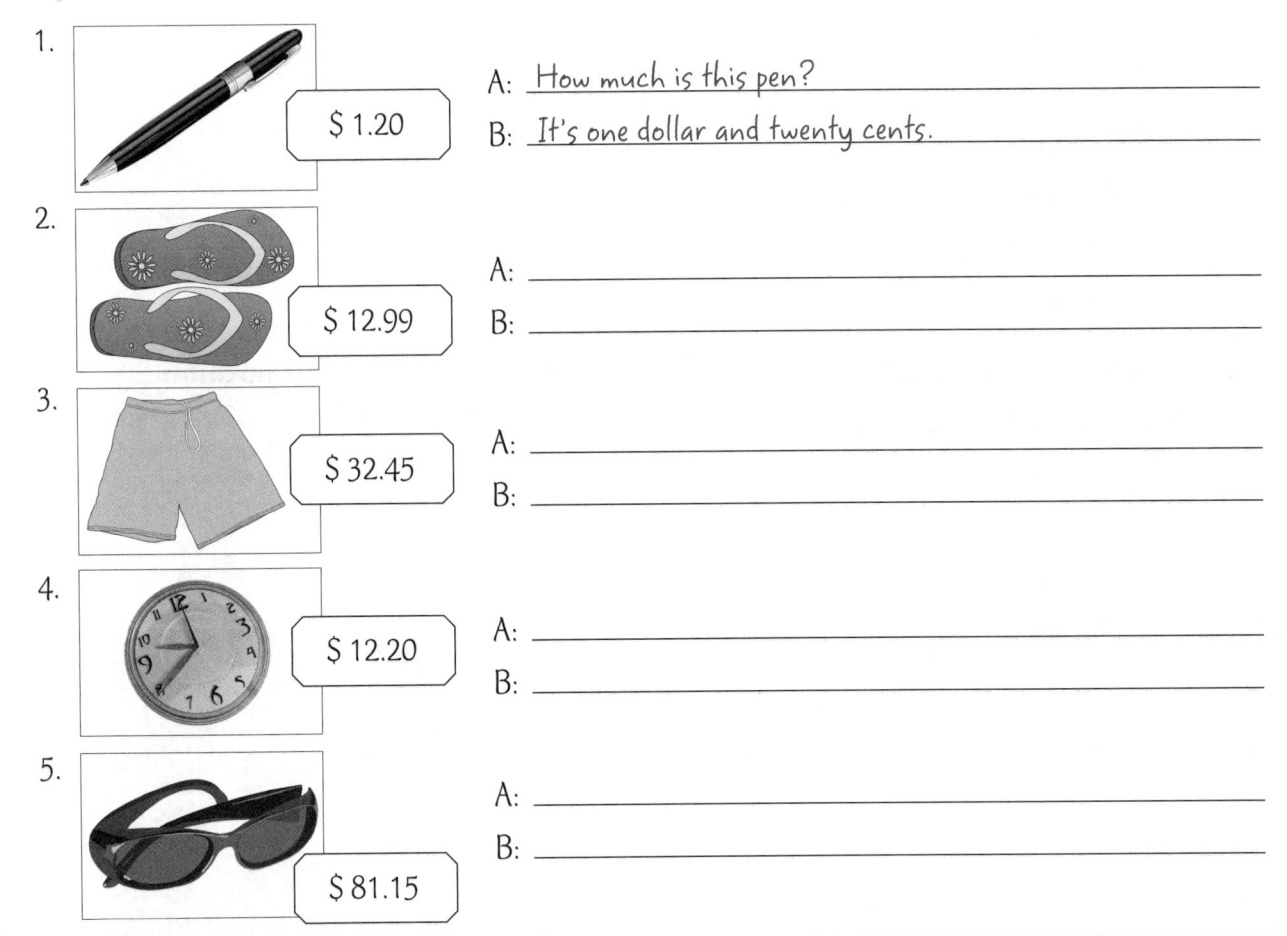

1. $ 1.20
   A: How much is this pen?
   B: It's one dollar and twenty cents.

2. $ 12.99
   A: _____
   B: _____

3. $ 32.45
   A: _____
   B: _____

4. $ 12.20
   A: _____
   B: _____

5. $ 81.15
   A: _____
   B: _____

123

UNIT 4

1 Look at the animals. Complete the sentences.

1. The zebra is in front of _the koala_____ .
2. The panda is behind _____ .
3. The cat is between _____ and _____ .
4. The macaw is on _____ .
5. The horse is _____ the cat.
6. The elephant is _____ the cat.

2 Look at the animals again. Complete the sentences about their position.

1. The zebra is _the first animal_____ .
2. The panda is _____ .
4. The _____ is the third animal.
5. The cat _____ .
6. The horse _____ .

124

3
Look at the picture. Answer the questions.

1. Is Lucy in front of Ken? <u>No, she isn't. She's in front of Sally.</u>
2. Is Mickey between Sally and Lucy? _____.
3. Is Jane in front of Mickey? _____.
4. Is Ken behind Sally? _____.
5. Is Troy behind Jane? _____.
6. Is Lucy between Troy and Sally? _____.
7. Is Sally in front of Troy? _____.
8. Is Sally behind Ken? _____.

4
Look at the picture again and complete the chart.

FIRST	Jane
SECOND	
	Ken
	Lucy
FIFTH	
	Troy

UNIT 5

1 Complete the crossword with the names of the places.

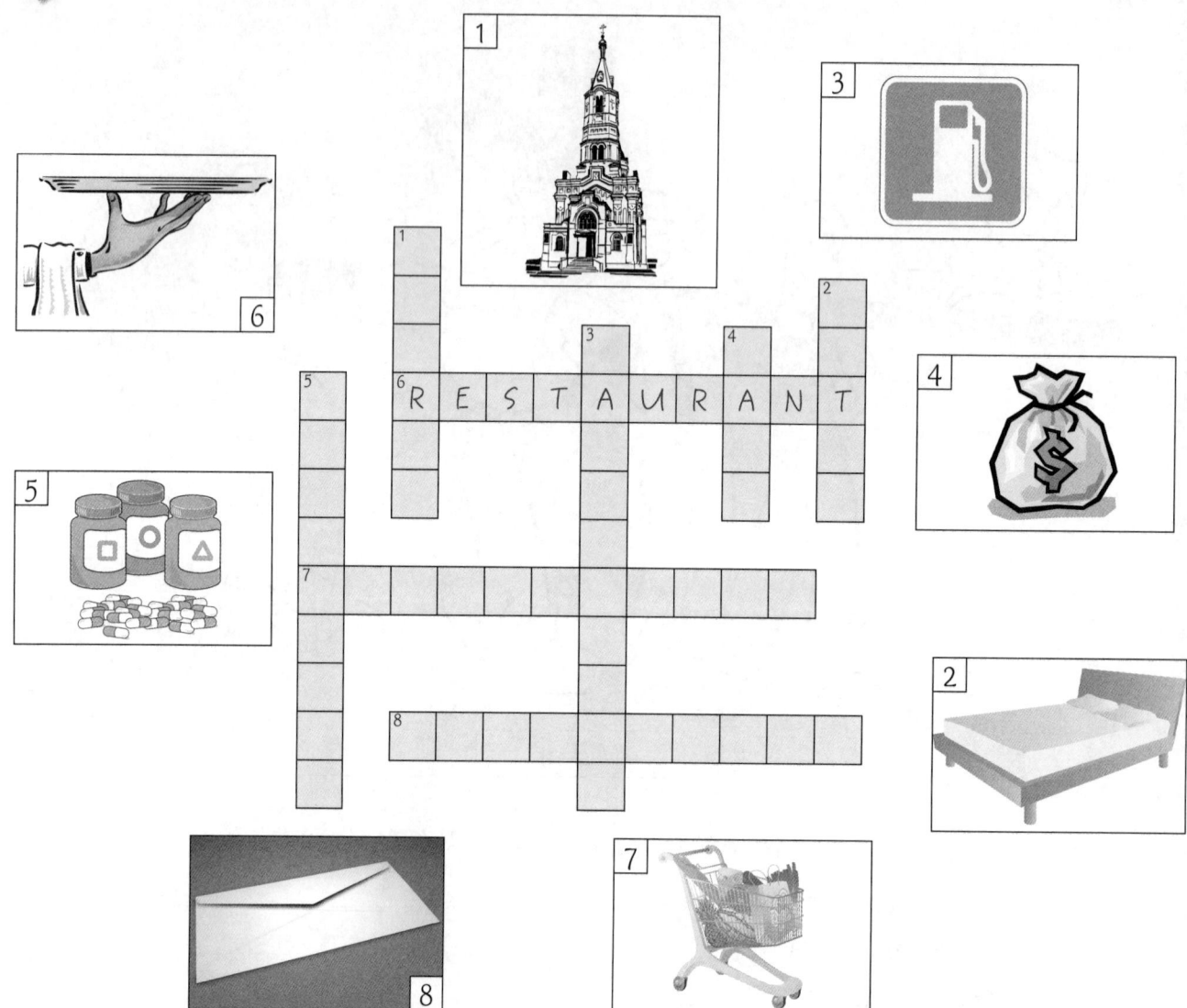

2 Complete the sentences with a word from the box.

| to | for | between | on | in | from |

1. The bank is next _____ the school.
2. My house is across _____ the church.
3. Go straight ahead _____ three blocks.
4. Turn left _____ Grand Street.
5. There is a small lake _____ the park.
6. The drugstore is _____ the bank and the hospital.

3 Look at the map. Complete the dialogs.

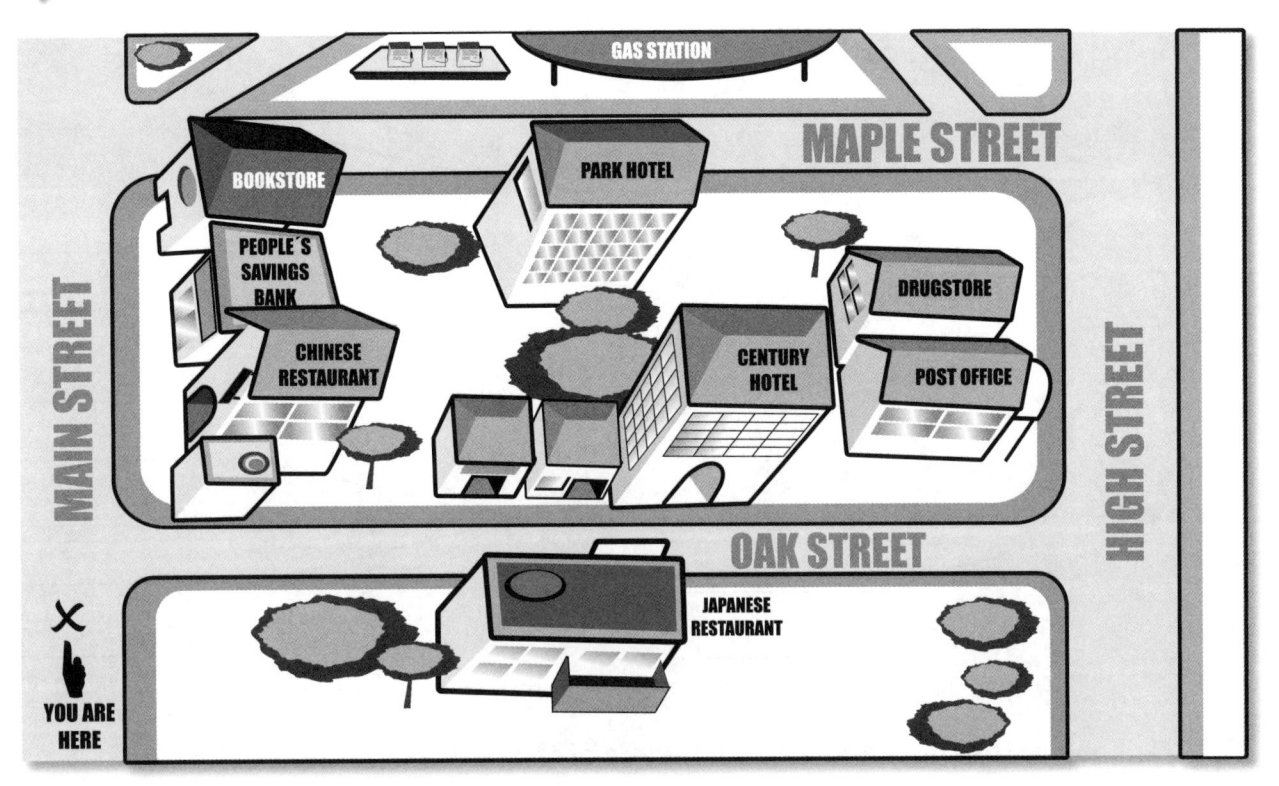

1. A: Excuse _me. Where's_ the drugstore?

   B: _____ right _____ Oak Street. Then left on High _____ .

   A: Turn _____ on High Street?

   B: Yes. The _____ is next _____ the post office.

2. A: _____ me. Where's the Park _____ ?

   B: Go straight _____ for one _____ . Then turn _____ on Maple _____ .

   A: _____ right on Maple _____ ?

   B: Yes. The _____ Hotel is across _____ the gas station.

3. A: _____ bookstore?

   B: _____ ahead for _____ block.

   A: Go straight _____ for three _____ ?

   B: No. _____ straight ahead _____ one _____ . The _____ is _____ to the People's Savings Bank.

127

UNIT 6

1. Complete the phrases.

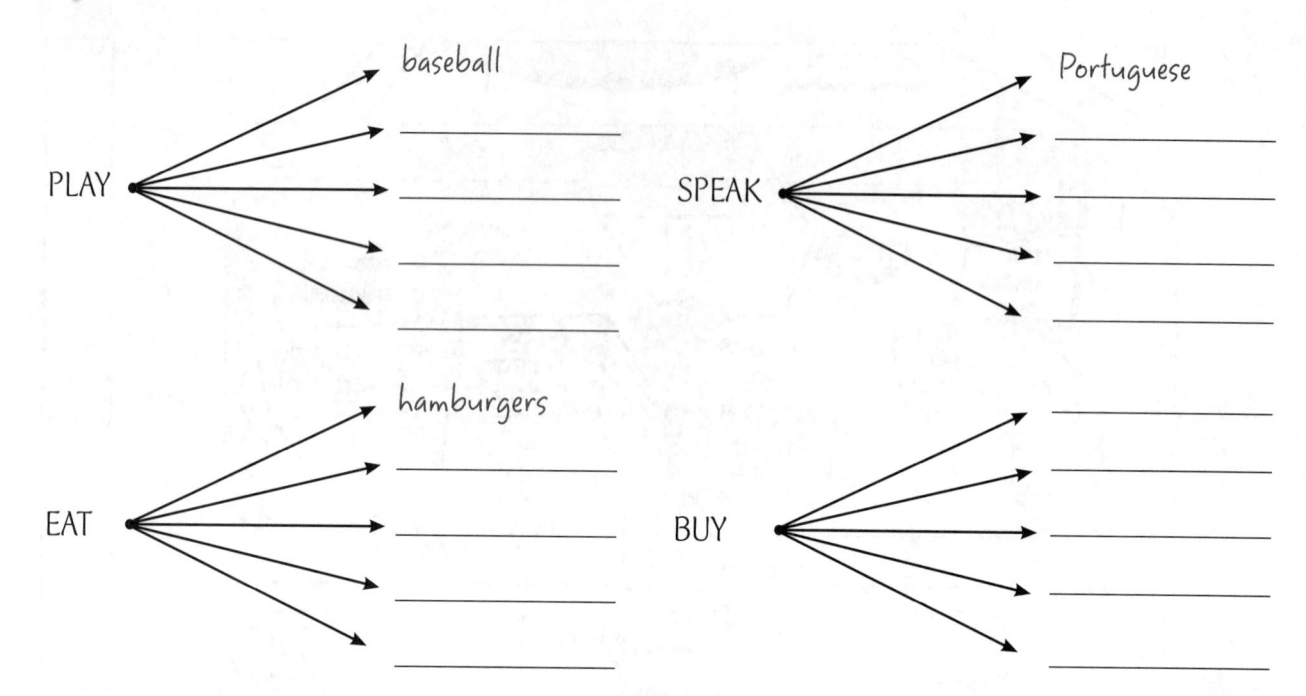

PLAY → baseball / _____ / _____ / _____

EAT → hamburgers / _____ / _____ / _____

SPEAK → Portuguese / _____ / _____ / _____

BUY → _____ / _____ / _____ / _____

2. Look at the chart and write the name of the person. (X = can't; ✓ = can)

	PLAY TENNIS	DANCE	SWIM	SING	PLAY THE GUITAR	SPEAK SPANISH	PLAY SOCCER
Matt	✓	✓	X	✓	X	✓	✓
Lisa	✓	X	X	✓	✓	X	X
Jennifer	X	✓	X	X	✓	✓	X
Tom	X	✓	✓	✓	X	X	✓

1. I can dance, but I can't sing. I can't swim, but I can speak Spanish.
   Who am I? __Jennifer__

2. I can dance and sing, but I can't play tennis. I can play soccer, but I can't play the guitar.
   Who am I? _____

3. I can play tennis and soccer, but I can't swim. I can speak Spanish, dance and sing.
   Who am I? _____

4. I can play the guitar and sing. I can play tennis, but I can't play soccer. I can't dance and I can't swim.
   Who am I? _____

3. Unscramble the words to form questions.

1. swim / Can / you? _Can you swim?_
2. cook / best / your / Can / friend? _____
3. football / Can / you / play? _____
4. Can / well / dance / you? _____
5. sing / you / Can? _____
6. you / Spanish / speak / Can? _____
7. Can / play / you / piano / the? _____
8. use / you / computer / Can / a? _____
9. play / your / friend / tennis / Can? _____
10. bike / Can / ride / you / a? _____

4. Make questions for the answers.

1. _Can you speak Portuguese?_ Yes, I can.
2. _____ No, she can't.
3. _____ Yes, they can.
4. _____ No, we can't.
5. _____ Yes, they can.
6. _____ Yes, you can.
7. _____ Yes, she can.
8. _____ No, I can't.

5. Answers the questions in Exercise 3 about yourself.

1. _____
2. _____
3. _____
4. _____
5. _____
6. _____
7. _____
8. _____
9. _____
10. _____

UNIT 7

1 Write the names of the objects.

1.  _____
2.  _____
3.  _____
4.  _____
5.  _____
6.  _____
7.  _____
8. _____

2 Write dialogs about the pictures in Exercise 1.

1. (Maria)   A: <u>Whose dress is this?</u>
   B: <u>It's Maria's.</u>

2. (Peter)   A: _____
   B: _____

3. (Jake)   A: _____
   B: _____

4. (Mario)   A: _____
   B: _____

5. (Priscilla)   A: _____
   B: _____

6. (Andrea)   A: _____
   B: _____

7. (Roy)   A: _____
   B: _____

8. (Daniel)   A: _____
   B: _____

3 Look at the pictures. Complete the dialogs.

1. A: __Whose__ desk is __this__?
   B: It's __Samuel's__.
   A: And is this __his__ umbrella?
   B: No, it __isn't__. It's __Joanna's__.

2. A: _____ keys are _____?
   B: They're _____.
   A: And are _____ her glasses?
   B: No, they _____. They're _____.

3. A: _____ pencil _____ this?
   B: _____ Samuel's.
   A: And _____ these his keys?
   B: No, _____ _____. They're _____.

4. A: Whose book _____ _____?
   B: It's _____.
   A: And _____ this _____ pencil?
   B: No, _____ isn't. It's _____.

5. A: _____ pants _____ _____?
   B: They're _____.
   A: And _____ this _____ notebook?
   B: No, it _____. _____ _____.

131

UNIT 8

1. Combine the words to make phrases.

> ~~history~~   in class   a book   a picture
> your homework   Spanish   on the phone   a magazine   to the teacher
> a map   exercises   geography   the dishes

DOING	READING	TALKING	STUDYING	DRAWING	SPEAKING
			history		

2. Underline the mistake and correct the sentences. Three sentences are correct.

1. I am <u>drink</u> milk now. _I am drinking milk now._
2. She talking on the phone. _____
3. He's listen to the radio in the evenings. _____
4. Sandra is reading a nice book. _____
5. We are go to school every day. _____
6. They always eat tacos for lunch. _____
7. They being playing tennis. _____
8. He is no watching TV. _____
9. They speak French very well. _____
10. She isn't draw a picture now. _____
11. Ken have lunch at home. _____
12. We read a magazine now. _____

3. Circle the word that is different.

1. beaver   toucan   (book)   flamingo
2. dancing   talking   singing   speaking
3. flute   radio   tennis   guitar
4. draw   dancing   eating   singing
5. book   letter   newspaper   apple
6. speak   geography   study   listen
7. legs   wings   ears   giraffe

4 Look at the pictures. Write dialogs.

1. A: What's she doing?
   B: She's eating a sandwich.

2. A: _____
   B: _____

3. A: _____
   B: _____

4. A: _____
   B: _____

5. A: _____
   B: _____

6. A: _____
   B: _____

7. A: _____
   B: _____

8. A: _____
   B: _____

UNIT 9

1. Match the food with the pictures.

1. beans
2. cereal
3. chicken
4. eggs
5. fish
6. French fries
7. hamburger
8. hot dog
9. rice
10. salad
11. soup
12. tacos

1. _b_ 2. ____ 3. ____ 4. ____ 5. ____ 6. ____
7. ____ 8. ____ 9. ____ 10. ____ 11. ____ 12. ____

2. Answer the questions about yourself.

1. What do you eat for breakfast? _____
2. What do you drink at lunch? _____
3. What do you eat for dinner? _____
4. Do you like fish? _____
5. Do you like salad? _____
6. Does your best friend like French fries? _____
7. Does your best friend like rice and beans? _____
8. What does your best friend eat for lunch? _____
9. Do you prefer hot dogs or hamburgers? _____
10. Do you like beans for breakfast? _____
11. What does your teacher eat for lunch? _____
12. Do your friends like French fries? _____

134

3 Unscramble the letters to form words.

1. Yoshi

   I like **maresghrub** <u>hamburgers</u> but I don't like **ifhs** _____
   I like **atocs** _____ very much and I like **hceknci** _____
   too. I don't like **irec** _____ .

2. Luisa

   I like **ecerla** _____ but I don't like **osup** _____ I don't like
   atocs _____ very much and I don't like **ebsna** _____ I
   don't like **hsif** _____ but I like **hceknci** _____ .

3. Paulo

   I don't like **gegs** _____ but I really like **spuo** _____ . I
   like **reci** _____ and **bsane** _____ very much and I like
   hsregrubma _____ , too. I don't like **eraelc** _____ .

4. Bia

   I like **tatos** _____ but I don't like **sdala** _____ . I like
   gegs _____ very much and I like **hceknci** _____ , too. I
   don't like **tcaso** _____ .

4 Read Exercise 3 again. Write the names in the correct place. (√ = like; X = don't like)

	tacos	eggs	chicken	salad	toast	cereal	hamburgers	rice	beans	soup	fish
		X				X	√	√	√	√	
	√		√				√	X			X
	X	√	√	X	√						
	X		√			√			X	X	X

5 Order the phrases in the dialog.

( ) Sure! And what do you want to drink?
( ) Hi! Can I take your order?
( ) You're welcome.
(1) Hello!

( ) Yes, please. Can I have a hot dog?
( ) Thank you very much.
( ) Can I have an orange juice?
( ) No problem.

UNIT 10

1 Write the parts of the body.

1. head
2. _____
3. _____
4. _____
5. _____
6. _____
7. _____
8. _____
9. _____

2 Unscramble the words to form instructions.

1. your move arm. _Move your arm._
2. nose touch your. _____
3. open eyes your. _____
4. your touch with hand left your right ear. _____
5. to school go. _____
6. to knees your point. _____
7. Bill Bob call and. _____
8. at look me. _____

3 Make the instructions in Exercise 2 negative.

1. _Don't move your arm._
2. _____
3. _____
4. _____
5. _____
6. _____
7. _____
8. _____

4 **Underline the mistakes and correct the sentences.**

1. Call <u>she</u>. Call her.
2. Look at he. _____
3. Call I tomorrow! _____
4. Her likes French fries. _____
5. Him has a beautiful dog. _____
6. Point to they, please. _____

5 **Complete the dialogs with subject or object pronouns.**

SUBJECT PRONOUNS				OBJECT PRONOUNS			
I	She	He	They	Me	Her	Him	Them

1. A: Sheila can't go to school today.
   B: What's the matter with ___her___?
   A: _____ is sick.
   B: Better call Mr. Smith. _____ is a good doctor.
   A: I can't call _____. My telephone isn't working.

2. A: Here is my class photograph.
   B: Where is your teacher, Mrs. Green?
   A: _____ is here. Kate and Mark are in front of _____
   B: Point to Mary and Bob, please.
   A: I can't point to _____. _____ aren't in the picture.

3. A: Wow, Joshua! What's the matter with you?
   B: _____'m very tired.
   A: Can you move your legs?
   B: No, I can't. Can you give _____ a glass of water, please?
   A: Of course!

137

UNIT 11

1 Unscramble the words to form questions.

1. time / you / get / what / do / up?
   <u>What time do you get up?</u>

2. school / leave / do / 1 o'clock / you / at?
   _____

3. class / time / is / what / your / English?
   _____

4. bed / you / what / go / time / to / do?
   _____

5. 6 o'clock / school / at / to / do / you / go?
   _____

6. school / lunch / do / at / have / you?
   _____

7. you / tacos / do / like?
   _____

8. there / how / are / in / many / desks / room / your?
   _____

2 Match the columns to create phrases.

a. have   1. _____ my teeth
b. get up   2. _____ school
c. wash   3. _____ dinner
d. leave   4. _____ early
e. go to   5. _____ home
f. brush   6. _____ clothes
g. share   7. _____ my face

3 Write the questions

1. <u>Do you get up at 8 o' clock?</u>
   No, I don't. I get up at 6:30 A.M.

2. _____
   Yes, I usually leave home at 7 o' clock.

3. _____
   No, I don't get to school at 8:30. I get to school at 7:45.

4 Look at the chart and describe Julia and Karen's routine.

TIME	ACTION
6:00	Get up
6:30	Have breakfast
7:00	Leave home
7:15	Take the bus
12:45	Have lunch
3:00	Leave school
7:30	Have dinner
8:30	Read and study
10:30	Go to bed

Julia and Karen 1. _____ 10:30 and 2. _____ 6:00. They 3. _____ 6:30 and leave home at 4. _____ . They 5. _____ at 7:15. They usually have dinner at 6. _____ home. At night, they 7. _____ and _____ .

5 Answer the questions about Julia and Karen.

1. Do they get up at 6:30?
   No, they don't. They get up at 6:00.

2. Do they have breakfast at home?
   _____

3. What time do they take the bus?
   _____

4. Where do they have lunch?
   _____

5. What do they do after dinner?
   _____

6 Answer the questions about yourself.

1. What time do you get up? I get up at 6:00 A.M.
2. What time do you eat breakfast? _____
3. What time do you leave home to go to school? _____
4. What time do you eat lunch? _____
5. Do you brush your teeth after lunch? _____
6. What time do you leave school? _____
7. Do you have dinner at 7 o'clock? _____
8. What time do you go to bed? _____

UNIT 12

1. Use the verbs in the box to make phrases.

> play   read   watch   study   clean   go to   speak

1. _play_ tennis
2. _____ Spanish
3. _____ Spanish
4. _____ TV
5. _____ e-mails
6. _____ the room
7. _____ the newspaper
8. _play_ the flute
9. _____ French
10. _____ French
11. _____ history
12. _____ school
13. _____ the beach
14. _____ magazines
15. _play_ volleyball
16. _____ a movie

2. Write the third person singular of the following verbs.

1. do _does_
2. wash _____
3. cook _____
4. read _____
5. clean _____
6. watch _____
7. study _____
8. speak _____
9. play _____
10. write _____
11. go _____
12. sing _____
13. drink _____
14. walk _____
15. see _____
16. dance _____

3. Complete the sentences with the correct form or the verbs in parentheses.

1. I _____ (study) geography on Tuesday.
2. We _study_ (play) soccer in the afternoon.
3. Larry _____ (study) French with Kim.
4. My brother _____ (cook) very well.
5. They _____ (write) e-mails every day.
6. You _____ (speak) Spanish.
7. Sheila _____ (clean) her room on Saturdays.
8. Drew and Ron _____ (go) to school at 6:30.
9. Your father _____ (wash) his car every Saturday.
10. They _____ (do) their homework after dinner.

4 Make the sentences in Exercise 3 negative.

1. _____
2. _____
3. _____
4. _____
5. _____
6. _____
7. _____
8. _____
9. _____
10. _____

5 Complete the table.

the afternoon   11:45 AM   the evening   the weekend
8 o'clock   the morning   five-fifteen   midnight
Thursday   ~~Sunday~~   Wednesday

IN	ON	AT
	Sunday	

6 Match the questions with the answers.

__d__ 1. Are you thirsty?
_____ 2. Does she play the guitar?
_____ 3. Can they speak English?
_____ 4. How many desks are there in your classroom?
_____ 5. Do they like salad?
_____ 6. What time do you get up?
_____ 7. What is this?
_____ 8. Whose room is this?
_____ 9. Is she Canadian?
_____ 10. Is there a computer in your room?

a. No, she isn't.
b. It's a ruler.
c. At 6:30 AM.
d. No, I'm hungry.
e. Thirty-five.
f. No, there isn't.
g. No, she doesn't.
h. Yes, they love it.
i. No, they can speak French.
j. Tricia's.

UNIT 13

1 Label the pictures.

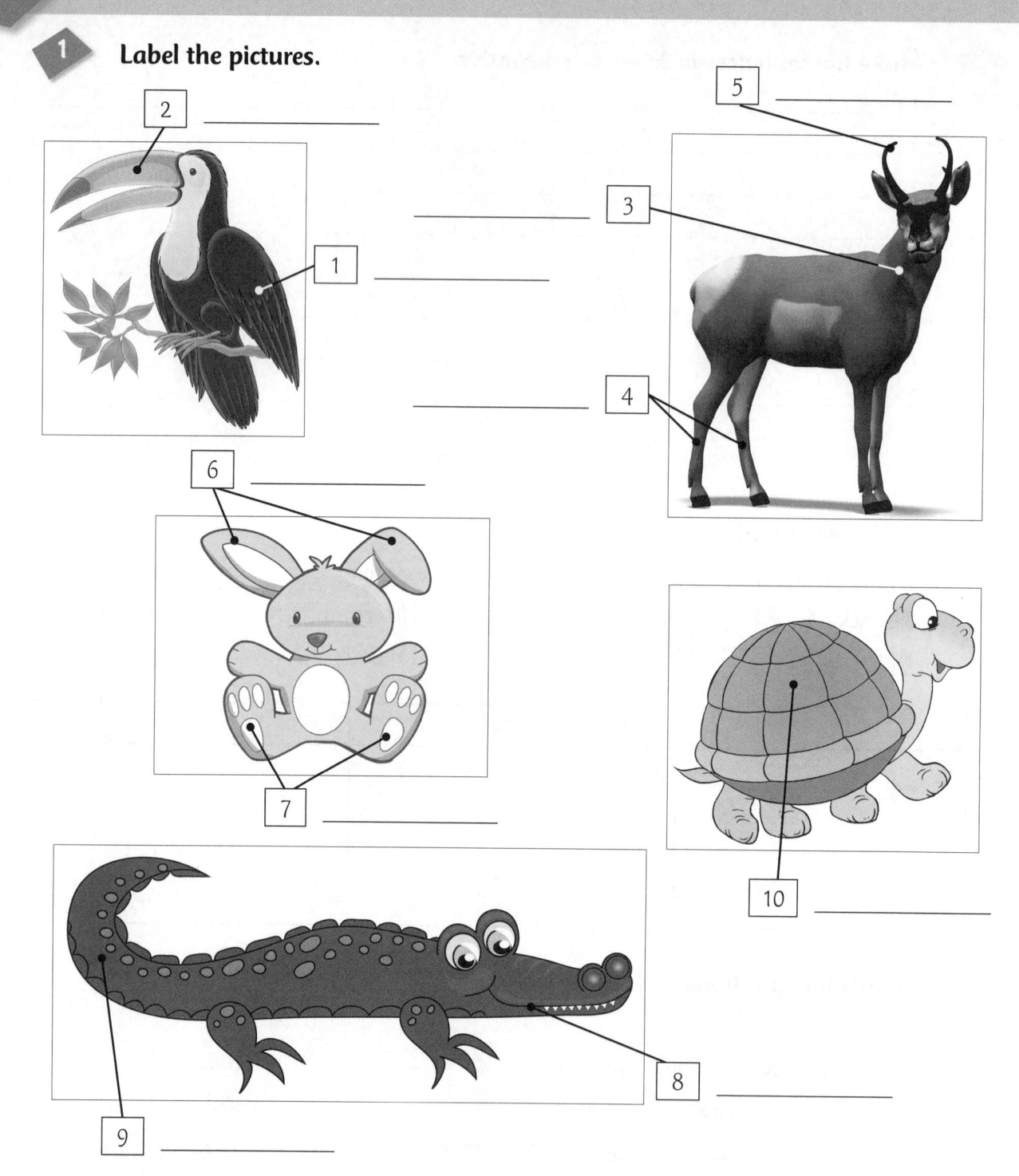

1. _____
2. _____
3. _____
4. _____
5. _____
6. _____
7. _____
8. _____
9. _____
10. _____

2 Underline the mistakes and correct the sentences.

1. A rabbit has <u>short</u> ears. _No it doesn't. A rabbit has long ears._
2. A giraffe has a short neck. _____
3. An antelope has wings. _____
4. A toucan has a short beak. _____
5. A flamingo has short legs. _____

3 **Write a sentence about each animal.**

1. turtle _A turtle has very short legs._
2. beaver _____
3. crab _____
4. cat _____
5. giraffe _____
6. alligator _____
7. antelope _____
8. rabbit _____

4 **Write questions and answers.**

Does	a/an	rabbit crab giraffe beaver antelope flamingo toucan	have (a)	long short small large	white black red brown pink green orange	legs ears wings neck beak feet horns teeth shell tail	?

1. _Does a rabbit have short green ears?_   _No, it doesn't._
2. _____   _____
3. _____   _____
4. _____   _____
5. _____   _____
6. _____   _____
7. _____   _____
8. _____   _____
9. _____   _____
10. _____   _____

UNIT 14

1. Complete the phrases with the correct verb.

| ~~do~~ | watch | set | make | listen | play | do | take | talk | read |

1. __Do__ homework
2. _____ out the garbage
3. _____ TV
4. _____ to the radio
5. _____ a book
6. _____ the bed
7. _____ on the phone
8. _____ soccer
9. _____ the dishes
10. _____ the table

2. Put the phrases from Exercise 1 in the correct column.

WORK	PLAY
Do homework	

3. Complete the sentences about yourself. Use *always*, *usually* or *never*.

1. I _____ do my homework.
2. My best friend _____ does his/her homework.
3. I _____ watch TV at night.
4. I _____ listen to the radio.
5. My friends and I _____ go to the beach.
6. I _____ make my bed.
7. My best friend _____ plays soccer.
8. I _____ set the table.

4 **Unscramble the words to form sentences.**

1. night / usually / Saturday / does / she / dishes / the / on.
   She usually does the dishes on Saturday night.

2. at / bus / I / catch / always / 8:00 / the.
   _____

3. you / breakfast / eat / do / when / usually?
   _____

4. your / lunch / does / usually / mother / what / cook / time?
   _____

5. garbage / you / out / when / take / do / the?
   _____

6. you / bed / usually / your / make / do?
   _____

7. never / TV / in / Sam / morning / watches / the.
   _____

8. Ana / does / the / do / when / dishes?
   _____

5 **Underline the mistakes and correct the sentences.**

1. Maria <u>is playing</u> soccer every Sunday.
   Maria plays soccer every Sunday.

2. They never watches TV in the morning.
   _____

3. Paulo usually do his homework.
   _____

4. We listen to music now.
   _____

5. Mariana doesn't studying now.
   _____

6. We write never e-mails in Spanish.
   _____

7. Carlos never go to school by bike.
   _____

8. They are usually play soccer after school.
   _____

UNIT 15

1 Look at the pictures. Write the names of the means of transportation.

1. _____

2. _____

3. _____

4. _____

5. _____

2 Use the cues to write sentences about where people are going.

1. Erica / the mountains / plane _Erica is going to the mountains by plane._
2. Ricardo / Fortaleza / bus _____
3. Sandra / movies / car _____
4. Patrick / London / plane _____
5. Barry and Tim / Greece / boat _____
6. Thiago / shopping center / train _____
7. Kate and I / the beach / car _____
8. They / school / bus _____

3
Look at Guilherme's family tree. Complete the sentences.

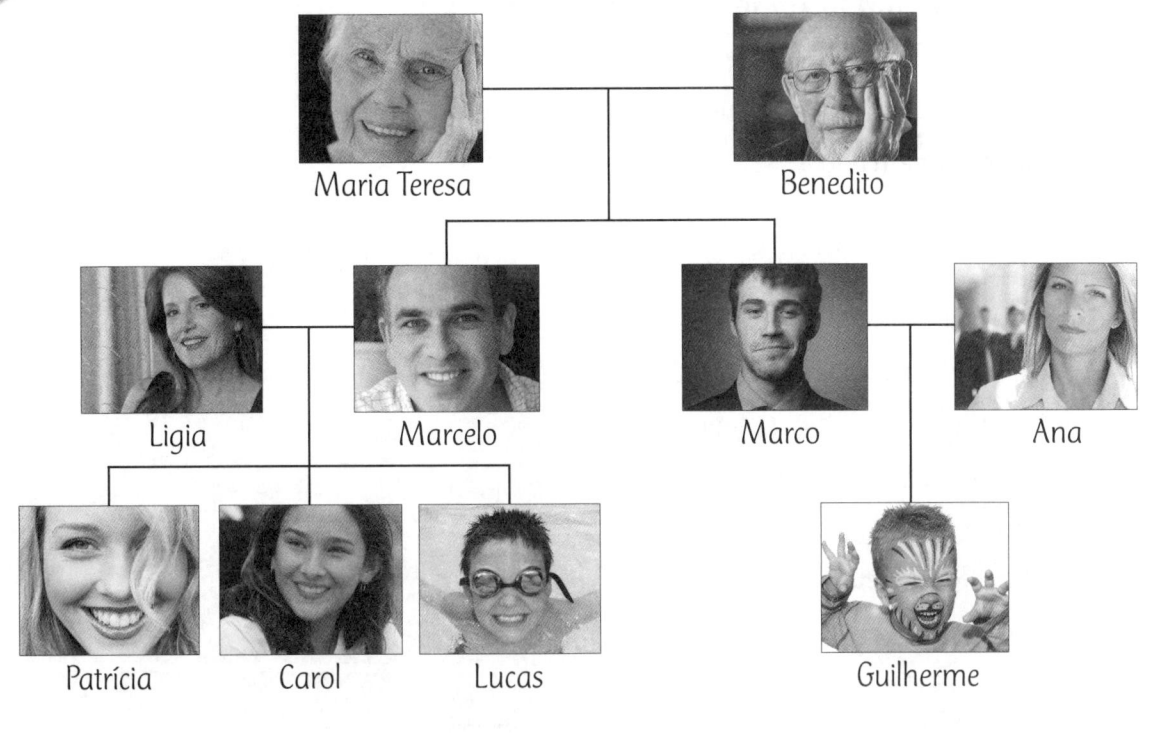

Maria Teresa — Benedito

Ligia — Marcelo   Marco — Ana

Patrícia   Carol   Lucas   Guilherme

1. Marcelo is Carol's _father_.
2. Maria Teresa is Marco's _____.
3. Guilherme is Carol's _____.
4. Ligia is Patricia's _____.
5. Ana is Lucas' _____.
6. Marco is Marcelo's _____.
7. Patrícia is Lucas' _____.
8. Benedito is Guilherme's _____.

4
Complete the text with the prepositions in box.

| on | by | in |

1. _____ the weekend, we are going to visit my uncle 2. _____ Rio de Janeiro. We usually go 3. _____ plane, but this time, we are going 4. _____ car. We are going to leave 5. _____ Friday night and we will be back 6. _____ Sunday afternoon.

147

UNIT 16

1 **What is Elliot looking for? Solve the puzzle to find out. Use the letters in the indicated column to complete the sentences.**

1. She ___always___ does her homework.
2. I never _____ milk.
3. A toucan doesn't have _____.
4. I _____ my father's car on Sundays.
5. A _____ has long thin legs.
6. He is talking on the _____.
7. A beaver has a large _____.
8. Do you _____ your bed?
9. She goes to the park by _____.
10. I never _____ the dishes.
11. What time do you go to _____.
12. It's eight o'_____.

Elliot is looking for _____

2 Look at the pictures and answer the questions.

1. What is Chris doing?
   She's washing the car.

2. What are Rachel and Diana doing?
   _____

3. Where is Pablo going?
   _____

4. What are Rick and Carla doing?
   _____

5. Where are Jane and Fiona going?
   _____

6. What is Derek doing?
   _____

3 Write the questions.

1. What's she doing?
   She's cleaning her room.

2. _____
   To their grandmother's house.

3. _____
   It's a camera.

4. _____
   Yes, I can.

5. _____
   By plane.

6. _____
   No, she doesn't.

7. _____
   Yes, I do.

8. _____
   He's talking on the phone.

Word List

UNIT 1

apple	maçã
appointment	compromisso
banana	banana
bicycle	bicicleta
boat	barco
bus	ônibus
car	carro
chapel	capela
dog	cachorro(a)
endangered	ameaçado(a)
enough	suficiente
farmhouse	casa de fazenda
greenhouse	estufa
guided tour	passeio com guia
It's enough.	É suficiente.
lake	lago
landscape designer	paisagista
mango	manga
orange	laranja
peach	pêssego
picnic table	mesa de piquenique
tree	árvore

UNIT 2

airport	aeroporto
aquarium	aquário
attraction	atração
bank	banco
calculator	calculadora
casino	cassino
cathedral	catedral
CD	CD
clock	relógio
computer	computador
currency	moeda
eraser	borracha
garden	jardim
heliport	heliporto
I'm kidding!	Estou brincando!
large	grande
magazine	revista
museum	museu
palace	palácio
ruler	régua
small	pequeno(a)
stapler	grampeador

UNIT 3

batteries	pilhas
Can I help you?	Posso ajudar?
cent(s)	centavo(s)
change	troco
dollar(s)	dólar(es)
Have a nice day!	Tenha um bom dia!
iPOD	iPOD
money	dinheiro
motorbike	moto
skateboard	skate
sunglasses	óculos de sol
video game	vídeo game
watch	relógio

UNIT 4

cute	bonitinho(a)
eighth	oitavo(a)
fifth	quinto(a)
first	primeiro(a)
fourth	quarto(a)
in line	em fila
Let me introduce you.	Deixe me apresentá-lo(a).
ninth	nono(a)
over there	ali
person	pessoa
second	segundo(a)
seventh	sétimo(a)
sixth	sexto(a)

Word List

tenth	décimo(a)
third	terceiro (a)

UNIT 5

a few	alguns (algumas)
bank	banco
block	quadra
bookstore	livraria
courtyard	pátio
cross	atravessar
drugstore	drogaria
gas station	posto de gasolina
hotel	hotel
left	esquerdo(a)
lost	perdido(a)
newsstand	banca de jornal
next to	ao lado de
post office	correio
right across from	no outro lado de
school	escola
side	lado
spend	passar
stairway	escada
straight ahead	sempre em frente
tomb	túmulo
upper floor	andar superior

UNIT 6

basketball	basquete
dance	dançar
drums	bateria
football	futebol americano
guitar	violão
help	ajudar
joke	piada
listen	escutar
piano	piano
play	tocar / jogar
run	correr
sing	cantar
soccer	futebol
swim	nadar
speak	falar
tell	dizer, contar
tennis	tênis
violin	violino
volunteer	voluntário
not bad at	não sou ruim (em)
Yours	Atenciosamente

UNIT 7

anything (+not)	nada
belong to	pertencer a (alguém)
boots	botas
camera	câmera
dress	vestido
fish	peixe
jacket	jaqueta
keys	chaves
pants	calças
tennis racket	raquete de tênis
tent	barraca
umbrella	guarda chuva

UNIT 8

ask for	pedir
8th grader	aluno da oitava série
bazaar	bazar
busy	ocupado(a)
charity	caridade
clothes	roupa
collect	recolher
cooperate	cooperar
draw	desenhar
drink	beber
eat	comer
everybody	tudo mundo

Word List

everything	tudo	soup	sopa
gift	presente	taco	taco
go away	ir embora	toast	torrada
help	ajudar		

UNIT 10

Let me see!	Deixe me ver!	arm	braço
listen	escutar	around	em volta de
look like	parecer	body	corpo
milkshake	milk-shake	ear	orelha
neighborhood	vizinhança	elbow	cotovelo
other	outro(a)	eye	olho
phone	telefone	face	rosto
radio	rádio	foot	pé
read	ler	hand	mão
run	correr	head	cabeça
some	alguns/algumas	jump	pular
talk	falar	knee	joelho
where	onde	leg	perna
write	escrever	mouth	boca
		neck	pescoço

UNIT 9

beans	feijão	nose	nariz
beef	carne	point	apontar
cereal	cereal	push-up	flexão
chicken	frango	right	direita
coffee	café	shoulder	ombro
eggs	ovos	sleepy	com sono
fast food	fast-food	stretch	alongar
fish	peixe	tongue	língua
French fries	fritas	touch	tocar
hamburger	hambúrger	village	aldeia
hot dog	cachorro quente	wake up	acordar
ice cream	sorvete		

UNIT 11

milk	leite	breakfast	café de manhã
orange juice	suco de laranja	brush	escovar
potatoes	batatas	catch	pegar
rice	arroz	come back	voltar
salad	salada	dinner	jantar
sandwich	sanduíche		
soda	refrigerante		

Word List

face	rosto	study	estudar
get up	levantar	tiring	cansativo(a)
get	chegar	watch	assistir
go	ir	worried about	preocupado(a) com
have	ter	write	escrever
home	casa		
leave	sair		
lunch	almoço		
share	dividir		
teeth	dentes		
wait	esperar		
wash	lavar		

UNIT 12

bathe	dar banho
begin	começar
bucket	balde
build	construir
clean	limpar
cook	cozinhar
do	fazer
dress	vestir
dry	secar
firewood	lenha
flute	flauta
go	ir
hang out	pendurar
household chores	afazeres domésticos
letter	carta
love	amar
maybe	talvez
newspaper	jornal
pile up	empilhar
pots	panelas
prepare	preparar
pump	bomba
read	ler
room	quarto
run	correr

UNIT 13

alligator	jacaré
antelope	antílope
bald eagle	águia careca
beak	bico
beaver	castor
because	porque
bright	brilhante
colorful	colorido(a)
crab	caranguejo
deforestation	desmatamento
endangered	ameaçado(a)
feather	pena
flamingo	flamingo
food sources	fontes de alimento
forest	floresta
frog	rã
fur	pelo
gentle	manso(a)
horn	chifre
hunted	caçado(a)
I guess	Eu suponho
leaves	folhas
less than	menos que
live	vivo(a)
live forests	florestas vivas
macaw	arara
meat-eating	carnívoro(a)
mice	ratos
pet	animal de estimação
poison	veneno
puppy	filhote de cachorro
rabbit	coelho

Word List

report	relatório
shell	casca
shoot	atirar
shy	tímido(a)
snake	cobra
soft	macio
tail	rabo, cauda
teeth	dentes
tiger	tigre
turtle	tartaruga
wing	asa
worm	minhoca

UNIT 14

adopt	adotar
anniversary	aniversário (de casamento)
believe	acreditar
bone	osso
breed	raça
do the dishes	lavar a louça
invite	convidar
make the bed	arrumar a cama
peacefully	pacificamente
set the table	pôr a mesa
size	tamanho
snack	lanche
stray	abandonado(a)
surf the Net	navegar na internet
take care of	tomar conta de
take out the garbage	tirar o lixo
vet	veterinário

UNIT 15

aunt	tia
beach	praia
celebrate	comemorar
costume	fantasia
cousin	primo(a)
grandfather	avô
grandmother	avó
mashed potato	purê de batata
meal	refeição
mountain	montanha
movie	filme
parade	desfile
pilgrim	peregrino
plane	avião
pumpkin pie	torta de abóbora
shopping mall	shopping
Thanksgiving	Dia de Ação de Graças
train	trem
turkey	peru
uncle	tio
wear	usar, vestir

UNIT 16

belt	cinto
blouse	blusa
empty	vazio(a)
give	dar
ice rink	pista de gelo
light up	iluminar-se
look for	procurar
pick up	retirar
post office	correio
present	presente
skate	patinar
take part	fazer parte de
teddy bear	urso de pelúcia
tie	gravata
Why don't you...?	Por que você não...?

Grammar Reference

1. There is / There are

Use Used to talk about existence.

Affirmative	Negative
There is…	There is not…
There are…	There are not…

There is a red car in the street.
There are two boys in the room.

Contracted forms
There is → There's
There is not → There isn't
There are not → There aren't

Interrogative	Short answers	
	Affirmative	Negative
Is there…?	Yes, there is.	No, there is not.
Are there…?	Yes, there are.	No, there are not.

2. Plural nouns

Noun + s	Nouns ending in consonant +y → change -y into -i and add -es	Nouns ending in -s, -ss, -sh, -ch, -o, -x → add -es
day → day**s**	party → part**ies**	atlas → atlas**es**
dog → dog**s**	candy → cand**ies**	dress → dress**es**
cat → cat**s**	spy → sp**ies**	flash → flash**es**
car → car**s**	puppy → pupp**ies**	sandwich → sandwich**es**
boy → boy**s**	daisy → dais**ies**	tomato → tomato**es**
		reflex → reflex**es**

I love my dog**s**.

How many **sandwiches** are there?

3. Prepositions

	Place	Manner
between	There is a dog **between** you and me.	
behind	The cat is **behind** the sofa.	
in front of	The red bus is **in front of** the school.	
next to	The girl is sitting **next to** the boy.	
across from	The hotel is **across from** the park.	
on	The post office is **on** Oak Street.	
by		I go to school **by** bus.

I go to school **by** bus.

Grammar Reference

4 Imperatives

Use Used to give orders and directions.

Affirmative	Negative
Go now.	Do not go now.
Sit down.	Do not sit down

Contracted form
Do not go → Don't go

Turn right.

Do not turn right.

5 Can

Use Used to talk about abilities.

Affirmative		Negative	
I **can**		I **can** not	
You **can**		You **can** not	
He **can**		He **can** not	
She **can**	play.	She **can** not	play.
It **can**		It **can** not	
We **can**		We **can** not	
You **can**		You **can** not	
They **can**		They **can** not	

Contracted form
Can not → Can't

Interrogative		Short answers	
		Affirmative	Negative
Can I		Yes, I **can**.	No, I **can** not.
Can you		Yes, you **can**.	No, you **can** not.
Can he		Yes, he **can**.	No, he **can** not.
Can she	run?	Yes, she **can**.	No, she **can** not.
Can it		Yes, it **can**.	No, it **can** not.
Can we		Yes, we **can**.	No, we **can** not.
Can you		Yes, you **can**.	No, you **can** not.
Can they		Yes, they **can**.	No, they **can** not.

He **can** swim.

Grammar Reference

6 Possessive case

Use Used to show possession.

Singular nouns → add 's	Plural nouns → add '
Tom's car The girl's mother	The students' pencils The girls' mother

This is Tom's car.

7 Present progressive

Use Used to describe actions at the moment of speaking.

To be + verb + -ing	
Affirmative	**Negative**
I **am** You **are** He **is** She **is** play**ing**. It **is** We **are** You **are** They **are**	I **am** not You **are** not He **is** not She **is** not eat**ing**. It **is** not We **are** not You **are** not They **are** not

We **are** danc**ing**.

Questions	Affirmative answers	Negative answers
Am I **Are** you **Is** he **Is** she sleep**ing**? **Is** it **Are** we **Are** you **Are** they	Yes, I **am**. Yes, you **are**. Yes, he **is**. Yes, she **is**. Yes, it **is**. Yes, we **are**. Yes, you **are**. Yes, they **are**.	No, I **am** not. No, you **are** not. No, he **is** not. No, she **is** not. No, it **is** not. No, we **are** not. No, you **are** not. No, they **are** not.

Are you do**ing** your homework?

Grammar Reference

8 Simple present HAVE

Use Used to talk about qualities or features a person possesses or what a persons owns.

Affirmative	Negative
I **have**	I **do** not
You **have**	You **do** not
He **has**	He **does** not
She **has** short legs.	She **does** not
It **has**	It **does** not **have** short legs.
We **have**	We **do** not
You **have**	You **do** not
They **have**	They **do** not

She **has** long blonde hair.

Questions	Affirmative answers	Negative answers
Do I	Yes, I **do**.	No, I **do** not.
Do you	Yes, you **do**.	No, you **do** not.
Does he	Yes, he **does**.	No, he **does** not.
Does she have a house?	Yes, she **does**.	No, she **does** not.
Does it	Yes, it **does**.	No, it **does** not.
Do we	Yes, we **do**.	No, we **do** not.
Do you	Yes, you **do**.	No, you **do** not.
Do they	Yes, they **do**.	No, they **do** not.

9 Simple present

Use Used to talk about habits, routines and facts.

Affirmative	Negative
I **work**	I **do** not
You **work**	You **do** not
He **works**	He **does** not
She **works** a lot.	She **does** not **work** a lot.
It **works**	It **does** not
We **work**	We **do** not
You **work**	You **do** not
They **work**	They **do** not

We **work** every day.

We **do** not **work** on Sundays.

158

Grammar Reference

Questions		Affirmative answers	Negative answers
Do I		Yes, I **do**.	No, I **do** not.
Do you		Yes, you **do**.	No, you **do** not.
Does he		Yes, he **does**.	No, he **does** not.
Does she	**sleep** early?	Yes, she **does**.	No, she **does** not.
Does it		Yes, it **does**.	No, it **does** not.
Do we		Yes, we **do**.	No, we **do** not.
Do you		Yes, you **do**.	No, you **do** not.
Do they		Yes, they **do**.	No, they **do** not.

Do you **play** soccer every day?

10 Object pronouns

Subject pronouns		Object pronouns
I	→	me
You	→	you
He	→	him
She	→	her
It	→	it
We	→	us
You	→	you
They	→	them
He likes her but she doesn't like him.		

I like **him**.

11 Frequency adverbs

Use Used to talk about how often we do things.

I **always** get up at six o'clock.	I **never** get up at ten o'clock.
I **usually** get up at six o' clock.	Do you **ever** get up at five o'clock?

I **usually** have lunch at home.

12 Adjectives

Use Used to describe nouns and / or characteristics of people and objects.

tall sad good important		
I am		
He is	tall.	He is a **thin** boy.
The girls are		The boy is **thin**.

The boys are **happy**.

159

Grammar Reference

13 Question words or information questions

a. How

How many books are there? There are three.
How much is it? It is six dollars.
How much are they? They are two dollars each.
How are you going there? By taxi.

b. Whose

Whose bike is that? It's Sheila's.
Whose sneakers are those? They are mine.

c. What

What can you do? I can sing.
What is he doing? He's watching TV.
What do you like? I like chocolate.
What time does your mother get up? She gets up at six thirty.
What does it look like? It's small and brown.

d. Where

Where is the cat? It's behind the sofa.
Where do you live? I live in Cape Town.
Where does Tanaka live? He lives in Tokyo.
Where are they going? They are going to school.

e. Who

Who is going with you? My friend is going with me.
Who is that playing soccer? That is my brother.

f. When

When are you going? I'm going in the morning.
When does Bruce have classes in the lab? On Tuesday and Friday.